DreamFields

DreamFields

A Peek into the World of Migrant Youth

An Anthology by
Mount Vernon Migrant Youth
& Their Allies

Edited by Janice Blackmore

CONTENTS

xi   Preface

3   Introduction

7   **MIGRATION**

8   I am from…

8   Chile, Tortillas, and Fresh Air

9   Los Olores

9   My Mother's Country

10   My Mom's Perfume and My Dad's Loud Music

10   The Sunshine State

10   My Noisy *Casa*

11   Crossing the Border

13   We are All Humans

14   Migration Interviews

16   The Culture of my Grandparents

17   The Morning When the People Came

18   The American Dream Rap

20   Half and Half

22   Skagit Valley Herald Editorial on Undocumented Students

23   It's Difficult

24   A Piece of Paper

25   The Promised Land

26   The Deportation of Diego's Dad

32   We the People

35   Venimos a Trabajar, No a Robar

36   Going North

39   El Jicaral, Oaxaca

40   Here and There

41   We Need Him Every Single Day

42   Shoot Me Dead

44   What If They Were One of Us?

47 FARM WORK

48   My Hands Are Colored

49   Suffering in the Fields

50   I Suffer but I'm Proud

51   Working in the Fields

52   Straddling Two Worlds

53   The Fields Are Better Than School

54   I Will Stay in School

55   The People

56   My Migrant Life

57   Struggling to Survive

59 STRUGGLES

60   Obstacles We Face

61   Desperation

62   Leukemia

64   Where Do I Do My Homework?

64   In the Bathroom

64   At Home When No One's There

65   On the Bed I Share with My Brother

65   At Home, But It's Really Hard for Me

66   En la Cocina

66   In My Crazy House

67   My Life is Difficult

68   No More Judgement

70   Theater of the Oppressed Scripts - In School

72   Theater of the Oppressed Scripts - At Home (Fiction)

74   Theater of the Oppressed Scripts - On the Bus

76   Bad Girls

78   Path to Graduation

79   Choices

80   Night Clamming

82   This is My Voice (Excerpts)

84   Like a Caged Bird

86   Domestic Violence

89   My Life is like an Apple Cut in Half

90   Illegal Love

92   My Obstacles and Dreams

95   REALIZATIONS

96   Responsibility

98   You See Me As Trouble

99   Learner

100   Mi Futuro

101   Estoy Aqui!

102   *La Mata*-Chickens

103   My Goals for the Future

104   My Life as a Migrant

106   My Family, My Challenges, My Life

108   My Migrant Life and Goals

110   Wrong To Worse But Then To Better

112   Eres Tu

113   Me Llaman Vivi

114   Prison

116   Brown and Proud

117   The Dove

118   Since I Was Five – a Rap

119   I, Too, Sing America

120   I Am Migrant

123   INDEX

Preface

What would we learn from each other if we had no fear, if there were no boundaries, no lines in the sand? As a society, we would be hard-pressed to know because we often lack the courage to do what it takes to find out. A dynamic group of migrant youth in Mount Vernon, Washington, are willing to try. They want you to understand what it feels like to walk in their shoes - shoes caked in mud from the fields, shoes scrubbed daily so they will last, shoes grown too tight, shoes carrying them from place to place. Their desire for your understanding is so strong that it overcomes fear, and they have decided to open their lives to you in a way that they have never done before. Prepare yourself for the soulful, powerful, and sometimes awkward writing of teenagers speaking from the heart.

Who are migrant students?

Migrant students move around because their families do seasonal work. They may be American-born, foreign-born, English-speaking, bilingual, trilingual, poor, economically comfortable, homeless, Caucasian, Mexican, Indigenous, Filipino, well-educated, or lacking in education. They fit into no clear category. They are impossible to identify by looking around a classroom. Yet, because fifty percent of migrant students in the United States do not finish high school, they desperately need to be better understood.

Migrant families in Mount Vernon, Washington, are almost all Latino agricultural field workers and most migrant students work alongside their families during the summer, with some also working during the school year. They most often come to Mount Vernon from Mexico (particularly the states of Oaxaca and Guerrero), California's Central Valley, and Eastern Washington. The students who created this book have all led a migrant life at one point or another, and most of them are still living it now.

Why do migrant students need support?

Migrant students need a great deal of support because they confront numerous obstacles to academic success.

"Social and educational opportunities are typically hindered by frequent moves, poverty, gaps in previous schooling, and language barriers. Poverty, language, and cultural differences add to the challenges posed by mobility, the identifying characteristic of migrant students. Moving from place to place makes it difficult to attend school regularly, learn at grade level, accrue credits, and meet all graduation requirements. It is also difficult to participate in socializing activities and create the social networks critical to social mobility. Mobility makes it harder to receive the adult support most young people need academically, socially, psychologically, and emotionally. Migrant students also confront serious societal and institutional barriers [...] the mandate to educate migrant children provokes xenophobia, from which these children require special protection."[1]

Frighteningly large numbers of migrant students are not graduating from high school.

"Research has shown that of all the subgroups for which data is collected, migrant students are one of the lowest performing groups. In several national surveys, data collected indicated that 49% to 51% of migrant students in the United States did not graduate. A 2010 Human Rights watch study, *Fields of Peril*, found that farm worker youth drop out of school at four times the national dropout rate."[2]

What are the goals of this book?

The first goal was to help the students understand themselves better. The accomplishment of this first goal took place during the creation of the book. The process of storytelling that this book required illuminated a path of self-discovery for the many migrant students you will meet within these pages. They have begun a journey, individually and as a group, which will continue long past the completion of this book. The second goal of this book, and the reason for its creation, is to shine a light on the often-unseen challenges and triumphs of migrant students, allowing the reader to better understand and support them, in Mount Vernon, Washington, and beyond.

Who worked on this project?

The students of the Migrant Leaders Club of Mount Vernon first thought of creating an anthology of migrant voices in the fall of 2010. As club advisor, I helped the students collect entries that reflected the diverse lives of migrant students. I also helped students record their thoughts on paper through both group and one-on-one writing sessions. Teachers heard about the project and

---

1   Green, Paul E. "The Undocumented: Educating the Children of Migrant Workers in America." *Bilingual Research Journal*. 27.1 (2003): 51-52.
2   "Office of Educational Improvement and Innovation Program Brief on Migrant Education (Title I-C)." *Oregon Department of Education*. Web. 28 Dec 2011.

began to share writings they had received in class, or writings of their own. Community members became excited about the book. They told us how the book could help them with their work in the migrant community, gave us feedback on our initial drafts, and contributed stories to the book.

As the students persistently pushed and prodded me, I compiled, organized, and edited the entries until we finally held a book in our hands. As you read this book that the migrant students nurtured into being, listen carefully as they whisper their stories, their truths.

Janice Blackmore
Migrant Leaders Club Advisor
March 2012

Some names have been changed, and photographs omitted, in order to protect students' identities.

"You may have a difference of opinion, but you cannot deny someone's story."

-- Naomi Shihab Nye

DreamFields

Some Members of the Migrant Leaders Club. October 2011
(Top row left to right) Guadalupe, Luis, Martha, Stephanie
(Middle row) Agustín, Ms. Blackmore, Alondra, Lucía
(Bottom row) Yesica, Ana, José, Cilviana, Thalia

Introduction

At the beginning of the 2010 school year, we decided that we wanted to do something big.

Something incredibly unexpected had happened to some of us migrant students that summer, and for the first time we felt like we could all do anything, go anywhere, and be anyone.

If you can believe it (because we couldn't), several members of our Migrant Leaders Club received scholarships and spent a week in Washington, DC. That same summer, another member of our club received a scholarship to spend a week studying with NASA astronauts in Alabama. We all headed back to work in the fields immediately upon our return, but we came back feeling like we were worth more in this world, and we began to have hope for the future. Our newfound hope turned out to be quite contagious.

When our Migrant Leaders Club came together in the fall, about fifteen of us from two middle schools spent some time discussing stereotypes about migrant students and how they were bringing us down. We realized that our voices had value and that we could educate others (teachers, students, community members, and our own families) about what it feels like to walk in our shoes. We decided to write about our everyday emotions in an attempt to make a difference in this world and create a better future for all migrant students.

We made a plan, asked for help, and never looked back.

Our Plan

- First we must create a group of leaders. All must know their history, some politics, and write poems or short speeches.
- Second, we must make a book of all our writings, which we will give to important people and ask if they would like to make a donation.
- Third, we must make ourselves better at speaking publicly. We should send papers to different schools and groups so some of us can speak out and start making a change.
- Fourth, once we start making a change, as much as we can, we should go to important events or try to speak to mayors, senators, and/or even the President.
- Besides writing and speaking out, we should go and take pictures of people working in the fields, for a face is worth a thousand words.

- We must stay up-to-date with world news, study laws and Hispanic history, and speak from our hearts.
- We are all leaders in this group; therefore no one has the right to tell someone what s/he must do, for this will only lead to a fight.
- We accept any person that commits to work alongside us.
- We must be humble.
- Most importantly, we all must have a dream. No one must say only, "Oh, I wanna go to college, I wanna have a good job, I wanna be rich, I wanna have a good life;" because all these are good dreams, but they are lame. We must have a dream where even though everyone might criticize us, once we make it, everyone is going to say, "I always believed in you!" Remember Don Quixote: *"Si los perros ladran, es porque avanzamos!"* (If the dogs are barking, it means we are advancing.)

What we did not realize when we began this project was just how much the act of writing would bring us relief from our suffering. Surprisingly, in our attempt to help others, we ended up helping ourselves.

If you are a migrant student, you may identify with some of these writings. If so, we understand your challenges and we have one piece of advice –let the world know how you feel.

With both faith and fear, we open our hearts and lives to you on the following pages.

Migrant Leaders Club
Mount Vernon, Washington
March 2012

illustration by Fidel and Rogelia. 15 and 13 years old. March 2011

Migration

"We didn't cross the border, the border crossed us."

—Contemporary chant referring to the US seizure of Mexican lands
during the Mexican-American War

In these poems, migrant students explore who they are and where they come from.
All were written in an ESL Social Studies class or at a Latino Leadership Conference.

I am from...

Chile, Tortillas, and Fresh Air
by Mayra. 14 years old. October 2011

I am from the deep green mountain of Santa Catarina
From the smell of chile, tortillas, and fresh air
And from solitude, silence and fear
I am from the stone *comal* of my *abuelos*
From the sweet memories of picking *elotes* in the wilderness
From Aunt Angelina and Uncle Reynaldo
I am from Hip-hop, *Bandas* and *Corridos*
From *"Ojala que nos vaya bien"*
And *"Mi chaparrita"*
I am from gathering with my family
From laughing with my cousins
From long walks and talks
I am from warm sweet *atole*
Delicioso posole
Exquisite *atole*
I am from those moments of the smell of chile, tortillas, and fresh air.

Los Olores
(Aromas)
by Jonathan. 14 years old. May 2011

Soy Jonathan.
Vengo de Baja California.
Una parte que a mi me gustó
era el olor a fuego que
había en ese lugar.

El olor de llanta quemada
el olor de la fresa
el olor de la tierra
que cuando viene el viento
huele muy bien.

I am Jonathan.
I come from Baja California
One thing that I liked
Was the smell of fire there.

The smell of burning tires
The smell of strawberries
The smell of the earth
When the wind comes
It smells really good.

My Mother's Country
by Elissa. 14 years old. May 2011

I am from Baja California, Mexico.

The country where my mom grew up,
Walking on rocky roads with no shoes,
All by herself looking for wood to use for cooking.
Only a little girl and she knew how to make tortillas.

I am from a family that's poor but happy.
I am from a culture where people love spicy foods.
I am from a house with noisy children.
I am from a family that makes amazing memories.
I am proud of where I am from.

My Mom's Perfume and My Dad's Loud Music
by Yesica. 14 years old. May 2011

I am from my laptop and games
I am from cars, plants, and bikes
I am from my first birthday cake and my mom's perfume
I am from a memory box and childhood pictures
I am from birds chirping and my dad's loud music
I am from Mexican people and Stanfords
I am from the saying, "I want you to be someone more than who I am".

The Sunshine State
by Cilviana. 14 years old. May 2001

I am from the sunshine state (California),
filled with people walking on the streets, making me feel no different.
I am from my mom, friends, teachers.
I am from the strawberries and blueberries filling my bucket.
I am the one who will help my mom.
I am the one who will make a difference.

My Noisy *Casa*
by Teresa. 14 years old. May 2011

I am from a very noisy *casa*.
I am from green trees beside my house.
I am from my brother who reminds me of my *abuelito*.
I am from a family that would always say don't be a quitter.
I am from the smell of hot warm tortillas.
I am from the music and the memories in my mind.
I am from the sound of a bird, a rooster, and a dog making their noises
every morning.

One girl's story of coming to the United States.

Crossing the Border
Verónica. 14 years old. June 2011

I remember one day when I used to live in Zapata, in Baja California, Mexico, my dad came back from the United States. I was happy because I thought that my dad and mom finally came back to live with us. Then I started looking for my mom but she wasn't coming with my dad. I was only eight years old so I just thought she went to my uncle's house and I went and played with my cousins.

That day my mom never came, so I just went to sleep hoping that she would be with me tomorrow. That night my dad was talking to my uncle about some stuff. My older sister looked sad but I didn't know what was happening. I remember my sister hugging me and telling me to go to sleep. My sister woke me up that night and said, "Get up, we have to go where mom is." I was happy but my sister wasn't. She put my new pants and a big jacket on me and we headed down to a bus station. I couldn't even say bye to my friends, but I thought, Oh well, I was going to see my mom.

From there, we went to the Tijuana border. It took us a couple of days to get there. Then we got in a car where a guy was driving and he took us to the middle of nowhere. (Well that is what I thought, but it was actually the border.) We were about twelve or more people in the car. When it stopped, everyone was in a hurry and they were all whispering and throwing their bags of food over a fence and climbing the fence to get on the other side. My dad was carrying my little brother. I felt like we were doing something wrong but I had to go with my dad. When everyone in the car was out, the car just left.

We started walking. It was nighttime and I was tired after that long drive. We walked that whole night. I was scared because there was this weird plant that I kept thinking looked like a person and I thought it was looking at me. I asked my dad, "*Papá, cuando vamos a llegar?*" (Papa, when will we get there?) He told me, "*Ya falta poquito, hija*" (We're almost there, daughter), so I just kept walking with him. We walked for three days and two nights. At nighttime I would always sleep in the middle of the all the people since I was scared. It was really hot walking in the daytime. The fourth day we ran out of food and water. We were really hungry but we still went on.

The next night, while we were walking, we all heard a helicopter coming. Everyone was yelling, "*La migra!!! Escóndanse!*" (Immigration!!! Hide!) Everyone ran to where the grass was really tall and laid down. The helicopter

11

saw us running and turned on its lights. The helicopter was coming closer and closer to where we were. I was scared and didn't know what was happening.

It all happened so fast. The immigration people came at us yelling in English. They stepped on my sister hiding in the grass. I think they were yelling to get up, because everyone got up. My dad was mad and said, *"Hijo de su puta madre!"* (Expletive) They took us to a little room where they gave us some food. We were there for about two days while they asked us questions like why we wanted to cross the border. Then they sent us back to Mexico.

This was a scary experience for me, but my dad never gave up. We did this three more times. The fourth time we finally passed. Now our whole family is all together in the United States.

Two middle school girls reflect on their feelings about living in the United States without proper documentation.

We are All Humans
Dictated by Verónica and Carolina S. 13 and 14 years old. February 2010

Not having papers: It makes me feel bad, and I worry about too many things instead of taking care of my work at school. If teachers mention college or voting, I worry about my class finding out. I worry that I can't go to college, that no one will help me get there. Even if I can go to college, I will not be able to get a job. I worry that I will get taken back to Mexico. I worry about being separated from my family. Sometimes I get headaches from caring too much about all of that.

For my family and me, not having papers is not cool, because we want to go somewhere or to visit my grandpa but we can't because we don't have papers. My uncle lived in Oaxaca and they killed him and we wanted to go back for the funeral but we couldn't because my dad had to work so that we could eat and we didn't have the money. Not having papers doesn't let us see our family. If there are emergencies, we can't get there. We feel like we're leaving them behind.

The kids who were born here get more freedom. They can go to sleepovers, hang out with friends, go to the movies, go walking. We can't because our parents are worried that we will get taken by *la migra* (immigration officers). It's not fair because we have to stay at the house and clean.

People who have papers get to work, but the ones who don't have papers have to work in the fields. Even if I have the skills to work for someone, I can't because I wasn't born here, so I don't have the right.

How come some people get the right and others don't? We're all human. People have to understand that just because some have rights and some don't, we're still people.

We are all the same. We are all humans.

Migration Interviews

Jonathan's interview with his father

Where did you live originally?
Oaxaca, Mexico

Why did you move?
Because there was no work in other places, that's why we moved to other places to look for work.

Where did you end up moving?
Mount Vernon, Washington

Jasmine's interview with her mother

Where did you live originally?
Mattawa, Eastern Washington

Why did you move?
We wanted our children to have a better life and education, and we wanted to be closer to our family. Mainly it's because we wanted a better job and to get paid fairly, because we used to work in the fields and always got home and just slept. This happens STILL, but we get paid better.

Where did you end up moving?
Mount Vernon, Washington

Ruby's interview with her sister

Where did you live originally?
Uriangato, Guanajuato, Mexico

Why did you move?
Where I lived my village was too poor and my dad decided that he didn't want us to have a future like his. He wanted us to live happy and healthy.

Where did you end up moving?
Los Angeles, California; Forest Grove, Oregon; Portland, Oregon; Kansas; Idaho; Nevada; Mount Vernon, Washington

Agustín's interview with his father

Where did you live originally?
Oaxaca, Mexico

Why did you move?
I moved because I didn't have enough money, also to get a new job, to have a better life. My dad was sick so I decided to move so I could earn money and send it to my dad in Mexico.

Where did you end up moving?
Mount Vernon, Washington

Alondra's interview with her father

Where did you live originally?
Oaxaca, Mexico

Why did you move?
I moved to the US from Mexico in search of a job. I had to help support my family in Mexico and to earn money to build my own house where my future family would someday live. I wanted a better life and more opportunities.

Where did you end up moving?
Mount Vernon, Washington

The Culture of my Grandparents
by Fidel. 15 years old. February 2011

Dear Rosie,

Thank you for coming to our social studies class and sharing information with us about your ancestors. I learned from you how important it is to love and respect your own culture. What I remember the most about your speech is that you still have memories of love from your grandfather holding you in his lap while you listened to his heartbeat.

I want to tell you about my own grandparents. My grandparents are indigenous from Mexico. They are Mixtec and Triqui. I would like to tell you a little bit about them both.

The Mixtec people are an indigenous group from Oaxaca and Guerrero, Mexico. Mixtec is actually a Nahuatl word from the Aztecs. It means "Place of the Cloud People". My people call themselves *"Nuu Taishin"*.

The Triqui people are a smaller indigenous group from the same area of Mexico. They are fighters, more than the Mixtec, maybe because they are a smaller group and are trying to defend themselves.

Thanks for coming and we liked to hear about your culture.

Sincerely,

Fidel

The Morning When the People Came
by Julian. 12 years old. October 2011

My name is Julian and my dad, Miguel, is a nice person. He was just going to work the morning when the people came.

He's a hard worker. He works long hours even though he doesn't need to. He helps out other people at work a lot. He goes to church, and he's a good follower. As a father, he buys us clothes every school year, new stuff even though we still have it. He would take us to nice places to eat on Fridays when he would get his check, and sometimes to the beach. He takes care of my cousin Raquel, even though she isn't his daughter. He gives her food and buys her presents.

We really miss him. My mom has been crying a lot so far. My little brother Eric has been asking when we can go to the store (because my dad is the only one who drives) and when he is coming back. My mom's been asking, "How can we pay the bills?"

Normally I'm a hard worker. I finish all of my work on time. I put time into my work. And if I don't have anything to do, I help my brothers with their homework. I try my best to keep everything organized and help my mom around the house and still do my homework. But the last couple of weeks have been hard for me because I can't get my homework and projects done for school. I just barely finished my book share for Language Arts. It was a couple of days late. I can't do some of my math homework. I just barely caught up from getting behind during the time when my dad was taken.

My family has been sad. My mom has been the saddest, also my little brother. I've tried hard to make my little brother happy, telling him that my dad will come home soon, that he won't be taken back to Mexico. I try to help my mom get stuff done, get the stuff she needs, take care of my brothers while she's cleaning up around the house. It's really hard because I still have to finish my assignments on time, or else they'll be late and I'll be behind. I can't do all of this at the same time. Almost my whole family is sad. I'm sad too. I can't think straight and still do my homework.

Could you please let my dad stay here and not take him back to Mexico? Then my family can be happy again and not sad and crying.

Due to the support of his employer, Julian's dad was released and returned to his family.

The American Dream Rap

by Frank. 16 years old. January 2011

The life of an immigrant ain't easy. Parents and kids want to live the American dream. Some immigrants are now living it. Others we still in poverty. For those that don't know, I'm the son of illegal immigrants. I also got illegal *amigos* and I'm proud of it cause they make me feel a part of them. Republicans are against illegal immigrants. Migrant kids end up growing up without parents and they end up in the wrong path because their parents got deported. People don't seem to understand us. We're just here in the U.S. looking for freedom and a better life. But I don't see freedom

Frank in front of the White House

here cause on the news I see my people get deported back to their country. And the authorities are abusing their power. They don't seem to protect us instead they check our citizen status then they deport us. Why is the border patrol still trying to stop those that are crossing the border? When are they going to learn that my people won't stop crossing it? We're unstoppable just like the virus HIV.

Did I mention I'm a legal citizen, not an illegal? But I still suffer like one of them. I worked in the fields. I saw kids helping their parents so they could get out of poverty. I was criticized by rich white boys. Now I advocate for my people helping them become a legal citizen by walking out during school. During the summer I didn't go to school. I was working in the fields to help my parents get out of poverty so they could live the American dream. Now that's impossible for my mom and especially for my dad cause not long ago he got deported. They still don't lose the hope cause they know that I'm gonna get them out of poverty.

Obama made history in the United States. But I don't think that that's the biggest history. The biggest history would be to see a Chicano being the president, representing the immigrant, living in the White House, and keeping the United States much more united. Cause when Obama sits in the White House it seems that he lost control of his power cause the governor of Arizona passed the bill SR1070 that allowed the police to identify, prosecute, and deport illegal immigrants. This reminds me of the Holocaust cause the American police are like Nazis. This law created a spiral of pervasive fear, community distrust, and also increased crime and costly litigation with nationwide repercussions. Now many states look to Arizona SR1070 as a model for new immigration legislation.

Now to end this rap I'm gonna teach you a little bit of history. We are all immigrants. Americans emigrated from Europe, raped the land from the natives who already lived here, and then had the audacity to institute laws designed to keep it for themselves.

Half and Half

by an Anonymous Male Student. 14 years old. January 2009

I was born on January 1, 1995, in El Jicaral, Oaxaca, a very beautiful place. An American teacher told me that if a child is born on that date, the parent is supposed to give the child a lot of gifts, but in the place I was born people usually don't celebrate birthdays, they celebrate holidays, not individual birthdays, but community holidays where there are no gifts, but lots of food and dancing and a big party.

What I remember most is what Oaxaca is like and the whole place because I lived there for six years. The place is very wonderful; it's warm, there's clean water, and you may eat every kind of fruit and veggies from plants. I didn't buy fruit or veggies, I just went searching and found what I wanted to eat. I went hiking with my grandma and grandpa every time that they went to find food and we put up a camp there to sleep, then we would leave the next day. Nature in Oaxaca was fascinating to me as a small child.

I began school about the age of five or six. In school, I was learning Spanish. My cousin was also in the school and he was an artist and he was drawing two bunnies that were facing each other like in the mirror. It was the first time I had seen someone drawing and I had a feeling about it. I was excited and impressed.

My parents had gone to another place that was called U.S.A. I couldn't picture what that place was like. I heard a story that my mom got injured in a car with a driver that was driving too fast. She got a scar on her head and arms and my baby sister had a broken leg but she went to the hospital in Seattle and now she's ok. I worried about them.

I hadn't seen my dad living with me for a long time and he looked different when he came back to Oaxaca when I was seven. After school my dad came with a car and that was the time for my dad, brother, sister, and me to leave from Oaxaca. We got on a bus and it felt horrible for me because I hadn't ridden the bus before. Then we got in a car and it took about ten people to where it was safe to begin the journey and dropped us off in the desert. Some useful things that people carried included clothes, food, water, and blankets. I was scared because I knew that if people were caught by the *migra*, they would go to jail and would be sent back. The difficulty was that some people got their feet injured by the sand, rock, and many pointy plants or, in Mixtec, *iñú*. It's very hot in the desert and what can be seen from the distance are mountains. There is no water. Three or four days it took us to reach the other side where a van waited to take us to Washington.

Oaxacan people struggle to make it to Washington to work so that they can build their houses in Oaxaca and have a better life, but some live longer in Washington than they planned so that their kids can go to school and someday help their family. My mom and dad planned to come here to make some money and then return to Oaxaca, but we have been here for seven years now, half of my life. My mom says we will stay until I graduate from school, my brothers and sisters too, because my mom says she wants us to have a better job than they do. But my dad wants us to start working with him in the fields now so that we can help make money for the family.

I miss Oaxaca, but I like my life here and it feels good to be learning something new.

Skagit Valley Herald Editorial on Undocumented Students
by John M. Crisp. Reporter. October 2011

I've written about them before. They occasionally show up in my classroom after having spent nearly their whole lives in Texas, attending public schools, speaking English, eating American food, marching in the band, playing football – that is, growing up in virtually every way as an American. Mexico is as foreign to them as it would be to any Anglo.

They were brought here by parents who were not only allowed to "sneak" into our country, but were encouraged to come here in order to supply the cheap labor that helps keep the price of our fruits and vegetables down. We've depended on them. In fact, fruits and vegetables are rotting in Alabama, unharvested because of the absence of cheap Mexican laborers who have fled the state in response to Alabama's crackdown on illegal immigration

For all practical purposes these young people are Americans. But…they live in fear of being stopped for a minor traffic violation. Deportation to Mexico lurks ominously in the background.

Crisp, John M. "Perry may be in decline for stance on immigration." *Skagit Valley Herald* *[Mount Vernon, WA.]* October 12, 2011. Print.

The following is a speech that Tania presented to the Mount Vernon School Board in support of undocumented students. Tania was selected as a LEAP (Latino Educational Achievement Project) Ambassador in 2012, one of only two middle school students to be selected in the state.

It's Difficult
by Tania. 14 years old. February 2012

Good evening members of the Board, Superintendent Bruner, my name is Tania. I am in the eighth grade at Mount Baker Middle School.

My parents never received a formal education, but they made me want one. They try to help me save up for college, even though they can't. And I know it's hard for them because they barely make $800 a month together and my dad is very sick and injured. He has only half of his middle finger and limited use of his index finger and elbow from a bad work injury and surgery incident. He is diabetic, he is going blind in both eyes, he is having kidney failure, and he can barely walk because he fell during work and hurt his legs and a small part of his spine.

I'm trying hard to live up to my parents' expectations. I want to earn the chance to be the first in my family to achieve a university diploma, but it's difficult.

I want to major in business, communication, science, law, and medicine. I know that if I work hard enough for the next five years, I can accomplish my dreams.

I came to the United States when I was four. Every day I pledge my allegiance to the flag and I consider the U.S. my home.

A Piece of Paper
by Frank. 16 years old. May 2011

The people in the government do not want to give us papers, they do not want us to reach for the stars. Is it because they do not want kids to have dreams? Or is it because they do not know how it feels to work day and night under the burning sun with its rays making us weak and tired? Above all I think it is because they do not know the pain and suffering a kid might feel when he wakes up to the loud noise of knocking and of men arresting his parents and seeing them getting separated all because of a piece of paper. They do not know the pain of the kid that now needs to struggle to survive, to find a way to eat, and even feed his brothers and sisters. They can't even count the endless tears of sadness the kid drops. Why even to this day are people cruel to each other just for their color and the place they come from? They say they're better than Adolf Hitler, but it is still the common idea that they are better than others just because they are white or a different race.

This should stop before more and more suffer.

The Promised Land
by Julio. 15 years old. February 2011

I hear my people cry out for a better life, hear them shout to God that they are tired of the way of life they have. So with great hopes they go to the land of dreams, a land where they say that your dreams can come true, a land that has people from all over the world. But when my people came, they looked at us and said, Get out! They hunted us like animals.

I see sadness in my people's eyes, but also hope – hope that one day there will be no fights because of where you are from.

And I have seen this promised land, a land of peace and prosperity, but there's a lion guarding the entrance. So the only way we can get in is by working together, to love and not hate, work for the benefits of others and not just ourselves.

So I say drop the guns and bombs and pick up a white rose for those innocent people that have died for a good cause, a cause that is the way to the promised land.

The Deportation of Diego's Dad
A fictional account based on true stories
by Janice Blackmore. December 2011

Diego's dad decided to work late that day. Thoughts of the cold winter months with no income pushed him forward, even though his back ached and his hands were raw from the thorns of the blackberry bushes.

Diego's mom left her husband in the fields that day and caught a ride back to their apartment where her four children waited for her to prepare their late afternoon meal.

Diego's dad never made it home that day. Immigration picked him right out of the fields and Diego hasn't seen him since.

That was one year ago.

Seventeen years earlier, Diego's parents decided to leave their small Mixtec town in Oaxaca and travel 2,500 miles into the unknown, not because they were unhappy or looking for adventure, but out of necessity. They left everything and everyone they had ever known because there was no other means to support themselves and their future family. They left begrudgingly, with plans to return as soon as possible.

They followed in the footsteps of many of their relatives and neighbors when they walked across the U.S. border and through the desert before finally arriving in Madera, California. They never considered getting a visa because they knew that people like them were never granted permission to enter the country. U.S. immigration officials required people to show proof of home ownership, a steady job, and significant savings. Diego's parents had none of these things.

They began to work in the fields almost immediately. Their years of experience working the land in their hometown helped them to feel comfortable with the agricultural work they found, but no amount of experience could prepare them for the long, back-breaking work hours that were required of them, or the patronizing field managers that left them heavy with humiliation, or the suffocating limitations of living in constant fear of deportation. They assuaged these burdens with thoughts of returning to their hometown with enough savings to build a house and open a business. They dreamed of raising their children back home, where their children would grow to feel free and proud.

Diego's parents did not yet know that the expenses of living as a migrant worker in the U.S. would trap them in a cycle of dependence that would be nearly impossible to escape. They never dreamed that their children would spend their childhoods toiling in the fields, feeling ashamed of their parents' dark skin and "strange" Mixtec language, and wondering when their parents might be taken away. At that time, they still believed in the American dream.

Before his dad was taken, Diego was toying with the idea that he just might be able to figure out how to get to college. He carried this new dream fairly deep in his heart knowing that any number of obstacles could ultimately get in his way.

The seeds of this college idea began in middle school when he attended several leadership conferences for migrant students at the local university. These events were like an awakening for Diego; he began to discover his strength, his potential, his value.

Diego began to ask difficult questions. Why are people from Oaxaca treated so poorly by other Latinos? Why do the poor Latino kids get bussed across town? Why do white people think they are so much better than us? Why does it feel like undocumented people don't count? Why is there so much suffering?

His search for answers led him to take Mixtec literacy classes at school to learn more about his first language, the incredible history of his people, and the history of their persecution. His search also led to his participation in his school's Migrant Leaders Club. With his help, the club spent the year educating their community on the difficulties and limitations faced by undocumented students. Through their work on this project, Diego and his fellow club members earned the opportunity to meet with lawmakers in the state capitol about laws affecting Latino students, marking the first time that middle school students from Mount Vernon had been invited to do so. By the end of the school year, Diego and ten other club members found themselves on an airplane headed to Washington, DC, having received full scholarships for a five-day trip with the Close Up Program for New Americans.

When Diego stood in front of the White House, he truly began to believe in himself and in his dream of college.

After his dad was taken, Diego watched his mom cry every day. She cried because she was now alone, she didn't speak English, she didn't drive, she didn't make enough money to pay the bills, she didn't know when immigration, *la migra*, might come for her, she didn't know what to do.

Diego, as the oldest, decided there was only one thing he could do. He imagined himself dropping out of school, working alongside his mother in the fields, helping to raise his siblings. He knew that making it to his first year of high school had been too good to be true. He always figured that something would eventually get in the way of his graduation. He began to let go of his dreams, one by one.

At a young age he became accustomed to having little control over the direction of his life. His parents moved often and without warning, from Madera, California, to Mount Vernon, WA, and back again. Plans were made and excitement brewed, when inexplicably, plans would change. The needs of the family always came before the needs of the individual family members and Diego knew no other way. He found it best to follow his parents without question, without expectation, without personal desires. This worked best to avoid disappointment.

And so it passed, with very little surprise and only a small tinge of regret, that Diego prepared to leave school to take his father's place in helping to support his family.

But Diego's mom had other plans. A strong advocate of education for her children, she knew Diego would never escape the fields if he left school now. During the summers, she would watch her children bent over the strawberry plants, covered with sweat amongst the blueberry plants, scratched and bleeding in the blackberry fields, and she would think, "Not forever. Not my children."

So Diego's mother stopped crying and began planning. She moved the family out of the apartment they could no longer afford on her earnings alone, and into the apartment of her younger sister a mile away. Her family of five now lived with her sister's family of four in a two-bedroom apartment. Diego's family slept on the floor of the living room and tried to stay out of the other family's way. Diego continued to go to school.

Diego's mom could now walk to the grocery store and the laundromat. She had enough money for basic food supplies. She knew she could at least get through the next few months.

The kids began to spend a great deal of time outside of the apartment in an attempt not to bother their aunt and her family. They found new neighborhood friends and they roamed the streets looking for things to do. Diego had been mildly gang-involved for many years, a nearly unavoidable rite of passage in the poor neighborhoods of Madera and Mount Vernon, but his participation intensified as he searched for ways to help support and protect his family. Diego's father had always been the disciplinarian in the family, and with his mother's long hours at work and lack of experience controlling teenage sons, Diego found it easy to lie to his mother to gain the freedom he needed to be with his friends.

Diego's younger brother, a seventh grader, began to follow in his older brother's footsteps. Unlike Diego, however, his brother's decisions were made not out of a sense of responsibility to the family, but instead as a means to escape from the emotional pain of the loss of his father and the changes it meant for his family. Diego's youngest brother, a sixth grader, quickly adopted his older brothers' dark-blue gang clothes, street-roaming habits, and easy lies. The youngest, Diego's eight-year old sister, felt not only the loss of her father, but also the loss of the only other female in the home as her mom began to work long hours outside of the home in an attempt to feed the family. Her brothers became more and more absent, both physically and emotionally, and she found herself quite often alone. She spent a great deal of energy trying to please her family members in an attempt to keep them at home.

Meanwhile, Diego struggled to keep his grades up at school. He had no place to do his homework at home. With the television always on and the living room full of people, he could find no quiet place to study, not to mention the fact that there was no cleared surface to work on. He attempted to do his homework on his knees while sitting on the floor surrounded by people. Most often, he gave up before he even started.

However, there was one thing he found he could do despite the noise. He began to write raps. He wrote about the anger and sadness he felt about his dad's deportation. He wrote about the injustice of US immigration laws. He wrote about gang life.

He began to perform his raps at school events and recorded a few of them. Then he mentored younger students interested in learning how to rap. His success with rap caused his grades to begin to improve even though his situation at home had not.

Diego will tell you that his father is a good man. He raised his children to have strong values and he led by example. They learned to respect their mother, to work hard, and to always put family first. They never saw their father drink alcohol. He did not solve problems through violence. He broke no laws and he paid his taxes. His strength of character and leadership made his absence all the more difficult for his family.

Throughout this last year, Diego's dad has called regularly from his hometown in Oaxaca, sometimes asking for money since it is nearly impossible to survive in the rural towns of Oaxaca without money from relatives in the US. Crossing the border is now so costly and dangerous that he has not attempted to return. The family has heard many rumors about what has happened to their father in Oaxaca. They all suffer this emotional roller coaster without any way to know for certain if the rumors are true. They do not know what to believe. They do not really know what has happened to their father over the last year.

Diego and his three siblings now live with their mother in a tiny one-room apartment. In that one room, the five of them cook, eat, sleep, and live. The family cannot afford a car, and a driver's license is beyond his mother's reach because she is not literate. She must pay a co-worker to drive her to the fields every day, greatly reducing her daily pay. In an attempt to earn more money over the summer, Diego took a dangerous job in another part of the fields, far from the rest of his family.

Until his dad was taken, Diego's family had always worked side-by-side in the fields. Diego's dad controlled the pace and decided when they would stop for the day. Diego's mom offered a smile or a laugh when they felt too exhausted to continue. The children followed their parents down each new row of berries knowing that they each played an important role within the family unit. They each understood who they were and where they belonged.

Since *la migra* took Diego's dad away, Diego's family has crumbled. What was once whole now stands in pieces. On the brink of young adulthood, Diego feels uncertain how to best help his family. Fieldwork, gangs, and academics each offer solutions and continue to pull him in three different directions. If he does not commit to academics soon, the more immediate pay-off of gangs or fieldwork will certainly lure him away. If he leaves school, he will be following in the footsteps of many migrant students who have come before him. He won't be alone.

End the Wars

by Yesica. 15 years old. February 2012

It's been three years since Uncle Peewee died
Having him present every day and night
Couple of months since my friend's death too
My sky now turned black, no sign of blue
Thoughts keeping me up all night, thinking who's next
Lesson learned from my losses is life ain't perfect
Not concentrating in school living in fear
Fearing my family could just all disappear?
Parents could be taken away while kids are sitting at school
Teachers teaching them about justice,
Tricking them into following senseless rules
Learning about history but you never know when it's true
Never mention cops killing our kind, but I wanna learn about that too
I wanna learn why people have such sick minds
No difference between our race…when you kill, it's still homicide
Our race is to be respected cause we respect yours
Mexicans come here to work, not to start wars
Mexicans with no hope that this country will accept us
Turn to the gangs trying to get them to respect us
Calling themselves *sureños* standing up for Mexico aka South Side
It's not making anything better but at least they try
Blinded by anger, only way to find respect is to react violently
Faking they don't care if they die, while they're dying silently
Hurts to see a teen in struggle, not fitting in, no idea where their place is
Turning from good to bad because people in America are being racist
In the end kids take the insults and suck up their feelings
Earn revenge with fighting and stealing
It's all like the game "Follow the Leader", I'll give you a clue
You try something dumb, we copy what you do
So respect us and we'll respect you
You aren't high quality and neither am I
Both races drink water and both have the same sky
We all eat and drink, our color and traditions are just different
Trying to help you accept us but there's a limit and we're losing patience
We're brown, we work in the fields, pick your food, and I'm proud to say it
Without us here the food that you eat wouldn't be created
We're not asking for an apology, or for humiliation
We're just asking for peace for this future generation
I love my race like you love yours
Let's live in peace and end the wars.

A speech written for a debate class by a migrant student and aspiring politician. When he gave the speech in class, the student received a standing ovation from his teacher. He then ad-libbed the speech for 250 people at a 2011 migrant leadership conference.

We the People
by Julio. 15 years old. November 2011

Eleven score and fifteen years ago our founding fathers brought forth on this continent a new nation with the idea that all men are created equal and free. The Arizona Immigration law that aims to identify, prosecute and deport illegal immigrants is racist and inhumane. For our founding fathers wrote one of the greatest things ever which is the Constitution. Let me tell you the first words, "We the people", thus saying ALL people, not just the Americans, the English, the Natives, etc. It's we the people.

This immigration law in Arizona is supposed to be good, but in reality it's bad. Why? Well because this is similar to what the Nazis did to the Jews and any one they did not like. Right now we are suffering an economic problem and what better way to "solve" this than by picking on some one. In the 1930s, the German people were in debt, had problems, and what did they do? They picked on the Jews. And this is the same thing happening in many states today.

They say we don't pay taxes. Every time we go to the store and buy something that is taxed, we pay them. We pay taxes, we just can't report them to the government. They say we are a drag to this nation. When the Arizona immigration law passed, business owners suffered an immediate 40% loss in sales! Why not give freedom to others? Let's remember the great words of Abraham Lincoln, I quote, "Those who deny freedom to others deserve it not for themselves and under a just God, cannot long retain it."

When the first pilgrims arrived to this continent, they came here to be free. They arrived here for equality, because back in their country it was bad for them. We immigrants today come for the same reasons; we want a better future for our families. We want peace and things that back in our country we can't get, like justice. Since all we want is happiness, why do so many people want us out? Does not the law say that all men and women have the right to pursue happiness?

This country was founded with values, that God was the all mighty and that he created men equal and free. But little by little, Americans have lost those values. The American people are not bad, they are confused. For if you want to admit it or not, your government has blinded you. And slowly our own race is denying that they too were once immigrants and that they are Mexican or Latino. We Mexicans can be a great people and a great nation, but no leaders have given us that chance.

I was watching a show last night, and it said that during World War II, Adolf Hitler had said that if Mexico were well led, it would be one of the greatest nations ever. This is true. I mean Mexico is rich, but our leaders are stealers and my people are confused and ignorant. This is why we come to the land of the free and brave, for a better life and future for our families.

Now let me ask you something. How many of you woke up today and ate a piece of fruit with your breakfast? Guess who has to wake up even earlier and pick that fruit for you? Immigrants! I was reading an article and something got my attention. It said that immigrants are stealing jobs that Americans can do and that Americans are the hardest workers in the world! They claim that they can work in the fields. I laugh at this for it is not true!

First, immigrants don't steal jobs; they create jobs. When a large population of immigrants goes to a store, that store has to get bigger, earning more money and creating new jobs. An example is our local Wal-Mart.

Second, I laugh because yes, U.S. Citizens can work in the fields, but do you think they want to wake up at 5am and work until 10pm under the burning rays of the sun? If they do, they want breaks, more money, etc.

The employers abuse us immigrants. Where is the Red Cross or the United Nations to check if the farmers are giving us the human rights we need? Now don't get me wrong, I'm not saying that Americans are lazy. I'm just saying that you are better at using your brains instead of your muscles to make money. But slowly Americans have gotten used to getting everything they want and are becoming a bully instead of the peacemaker you once were. Now with this I say that everyone should have a right to be successful. I admit this is your country and you can do whatever you want with it. But don't be out harassing or mistreating others for just wanting a piece of the cake.

Another point I want to bring up is, who is next? When the first Americans came to this country and settled down, there were slaves to work for them without any human rights. Now we Latino immigrants are facing a similar thing. You are paying us lower than minimum wage at times, and we work hard under the burning sun! And after you stop discriminating against us, who is next? The Asians? The Russians? Who?

I know there are a lot of you saying that racism is not a problem anymore, or that it's not a big deal. Excuse my words but don't be so ignorant! The Arizona immigration law is racist; people in the KKK are still active and racist. Some of you might be saying that people make racist jokes and everyone laughs, again, don't be ignorant. I'm not talking about immature people saying stupid jokes. I'm talking about the big leagues: the government, entire countries, big organizations, etc. Arizona's government is racist for it is stopping anyone that they think is an immigrant. Who looks like an immigrant to you? Short, brown people better known as Mexicans. Don't be blinded by your government. God created men equal. This great nation was founded by immigrants.

Now I give you the great words of Abraham Lincoln. "I leave you hoping that the lamp of liberty will burn in your bosoms until there shall no longer be a doubt that all men are created free and equal."

*Exell and Julio right before their presentations
at the 2011 fall migrant leadership conference.*

Exell wrote this poem as a summary of Julio's speech on immigration, then read his poem immediately following Julio's speech at a 2011 migrant leadership conference.

Venimos a Trabajar, No a Robar
(We Came to Work, Not to Steal)
by Exell. 14 years old. December 2011

Mi amigo Julio
estaba hablando de inmigración
y nosotros no queremos deportación
porque nosotros los mexicanos
venimos a este país
que se llama Estados Unidos
a trabajar
no a robar
como muchos dicen
para que nosotros tengamos un mejor futuro
pero yo he visto mucho racismo
contra los mexicanos,
Por que? yo me pregunto.
Nosotros pagamos taxas,
pagamos lo que es necesario
como el amigo Mario
y déjeme decirles que la ley marque
todo hombre y mujer tienen los mismos
derechos.
Que no se acuerdan que antes
no podíamos votar,
ni hablar?
Pero eso a cambiando
porque el gobierno
ha reaccionado
ha pensado
que nosotros somos humanos también.
Por ejemplo el problema de Arizona,
ese es un gran problema,
eso se llama racismo,
y dicen que eso se había acabado
pero no, eso apenas empieza.

My friend Julio
was speaking about immigration
and we don't want deportation
because we Mexicans
came to this country
called the United States
in order to work
not to steal
like so many people say
just so we could have a brighter
future
but I have seen a lot of racism
against the Mexicans,
Why? I ask myself.
We pay taxes
we pay what's necessary
like my friend Mario.
And let me tell you that the law
states that all men and women
have the same rights.
Don't you remember that before
we couldn't vote
or even speak?
But that has changed
because the government
has reacted
has realized
that we are human beings as well.
For example the problem in Arizona,
that is a big problem,
that is called racism
and they say that it doesn't exist
anymore
but no, it is just beginning.

Going North
English Translation
Dictated in Spanish by Antonio. 14 years old. September 2011

My dad came north before my mom, around the year 2000, and my mom came about a year later. They left us with our grandmother when Kevin was two, I was four, Javier six, Juana seven, and Cristian was ten.

When my parents were still with us, we were living with my grandmother, my father's mother. We would spend days with my mother's grandmother, but then we would go back to my grandmother's, and on and on like this. When my parents came north, we stayed with my grandmother, and we only went to visit my mother's grandmother about twice a week. My grandmother's house was close to the highway and we weren't allowed to cross it alone, that's why we couldn't visit my mother's grandmother very often.

Since we were little, we got used to my grandmother's house and I felt comfortable there.

My parents didn't tell us that they were going north. My grandmother told us that they had gone to Tepic, a fairly small city an hour and a half from the tiny town where my grandmother lived. (It's a place where you can buy lunch, chiles, soap for washing, also they buy supplies for chores like brooms, mops, and soap.) After two and a half weeks, she told us that they had gone north, and we felt sad.

At that time I was thinking a lot about my mom because her mom had come here and my mom didn't know her siblings that were born here. Also some of her siblings had been left with *comadres,* people she knew, friends, but not family. I felt happy that my mom would see her mother and meet her brothers and sisters, but I also felt sad because she wasn't with us.

I had no idea how long they were going to stay.

I suffered when I saw my grandmother asking her comadres for clothes when we didn't have any. I watched my grandmother talking to her comadres to see if they had any clothes they didn't need. Also my parents sent us used, or semi-used, clothes from here.

I felt love for my grandmother because we stayed with her the whole time.

My grandmother started to tell us that we were going to go with my parents. We felt happy, but also sad because they had to work so hard. How could they earn so much money? $4000 for each person: five kids, two uncles, one aunt, and my grandmother. In preparation, my grandmother did everything, paid for the bus to go to Tijuana, everything...

The *coyote* (people smuggler) told us that my little brother and I were too little to walk across the desert, or to walk across the border, so we crossed by car with some adults. There were a lot of them in a Suburban, seven people and me, and Kevin went in a different car. I was sitting with them; I wasn't hiding. I was scared because they were people I didn't know. My grandmother put me in the car. They had me cross under the name of another person. The people in the Suburban left me with an aunt I didn't know who lives in California. Kevin arrived the next day.

Almost everyone else tried to walk across the border, but they caught my brother Javier and my sister Juanita and they left them alone, separated, for a day and a half there where they caught them, like a jail but different, Javier with people he didn't know, and my sister with other women she didn't know. They took them back to Tijuana, and from there a friend of my grandmother's who lived in Tijuana went to pick them up. The coyote said that it would be better to cross at another place, and that he would pick them up in a hotel. My grandmother's friend took them to the hotel where the coyote was going to pick them up. They tried again to walk across and they were successful in entering the United States. From there, they met up with the others and went to my aunt's house in California.

We stayed with my aunt for three days because my grandmother was crossing the border by walking alone across the desert for two days. Crossing by car is more expensive than walking across the border, and walking across the border is more expensive than walking across the desert. One coyote got us all across. My grandmother arrived with very swollen feet. She couldn't walk because she had run so much without rest. We just sat and watched her. She couldn't walk for more than a week. They had to carry her. Her feet hurt a lot.

When I arrived at my aunt's house in California, my dad was there. My mom was waiting for us in Mount Vernon. I felt really happy to see my dad because it had been like six or seven years since I had seen him.

Finally my dad took us to Mount Vernon by car, a van. I felt so excited to see him. When we arrived, we didn't recognize my mom because when we were little we saw her as so tall and when we arrived she was so short. My dad told us, "Go to your mom," and we said, "Where is she?" We didn't recognize her.

When we arrived here in the United States, the food bothered our stomachs and in Mexico it didn't, we were used to eating just Mexican food there. It was the same food here, but it made us feel bad and it didn't taste the same. Also here it is much colder. I prefer the weather in Mexico where it's warmer, not so cold.

But in the end, It's better here because my mom says that there you have to pay to go to school: lunch (if you don't have money, you don't eat anything all day), uniforms, supplies, books. Also there if you want to go to school on the bus you have to pay money, if not, you have to walk. We walked there all the time. Every day at school we ate one taco with beans. My grandmother gave us five pesos each to buy our taco. Another difference is that there you clean up with cold water from the faucet and we arrived here and you wash up in the shower with warm water.

I felt excited to see my parents after so much time. I still feel good that I'm with them.

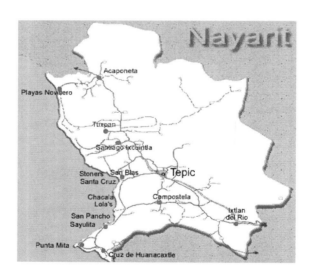

El Jicaral, Oaxaca

by an Anonymous Male Student. 14 years old. March 2009

If anyone wants to go on vacation, the small town of El Jicaral, Oaxaca, will be a really great place for them because with their rights, they can come back and forth, but for many of us, we can go visit, but to come back will be difficult. They may see many handmade works of art in Oaxaca, such as pots, cups, plates, and more. How would you feel if you missed out on all the luscious fruits available to you in Oaxaca? This is why El Jicaral, Oaxaca, is my favorite place.

First of all, El Jicaral is my favorite place because I hiked with my grandma and grandpa. We hiked in the forest and saw some animals that passed by. What I smelled in the forest was the fresh air full of the scents that flowers have and the sound that the trees make when the wind blows through them, also the warmth of it. Many birds I saw flap their wings flying through the forest with a lot of chirping and singing sounds from the top and everywhere around.

Next, while in the forest I could find food. Food can be found if you try to look for it. People usually go fishing and catch a fish with fishing sticks that are not long. Also they use some fireworks to make it easier for them to get those fish. Nets can be used to catch fish and shrimps. I like the smells of the soups mixed with fish or shrimp and veggies. Gathering food is an easy job to do because you just need to go out in the forest and pick some berries that come from bushes and vines or other fruits from stems and trees.

El Jicaral is along Oaxaca's Western border

Finally I thought swimming in the stream sounded fun to me because you could see the bottom and it is very shallow and clean. It's not deep or dangerous, but it's dangerous when it rains because the stream gets dirty and flows down fast. I like swimming because of the beautiful sparkling water when the sun shines.

In conclusion, I predict that if you visit El Jicaral, Oaxaca, it will become your favorite place too. Now that you know more information about Oaxaca, don't you want to see how magnificent it is?

Here and There

by an Anonymous Male Student. 15 years old. January 2010

My family came here for money to build a better home back in Oaxaca. Because there is not a lot of money there, we only have a little to feed ourselves. The little kids like to eat candy or want to buy something to eat but there's not so much money there.

But here we don't have much fun. There you can go out to the forest, go play, climb trees, have fun, or gather fruits to eat, but here you cannot do that. You have to buy fruit or snacks to eat. You stay inside more here. If I were there, I might go swimming or I might hike. Here, there aren't so many things to do. In my house, I cannot do anything, only just hear the noises that everyone makes in the house but not the sound of the beautiful creatures outside. I cannot feel the warm air, or take a nap in the shade, or go out fishing. I would like to taste the fruit that I tasted there, that I miss. Or the healthy food that they make there, that has not been refrigerated like here, because there we just went out and got it.

We Need Him Every Single Day
by Rigoberto. 13 years old. February 2011

My name is Rigo and I am writing to tell you about why I need my father.

My 16-year old brother and I really need him at home with us. He's the only person from our family that we have here in the United States. My mom doesn't live in the U.S., she was deported a long time ago. My brother and I don't have money to buy food or clothes. I don't have a winter coat. My mom has no money in Mexico and we are trying our best to send her money to buy something to eat, but without my dad, it's almost impossible. We used to live with our dad and we can't stop thinking about him. We need him every single day.

I feel sad every single time I think about him. Every day I think about him and I can't stop thinking about him and when I go to school, I can't stop thinking about him. Sometimes I just want to cry. I want to tell him not to worry about me because I'm trying my best in school, my grades are good, to not worry, but it's hard when he's not here beside me.

I need him beside me. Every single time I think of him I want to cry, but I want to put that aside and keep trying my best so that he won't have to worry about me.

Please don't keep him inside the jail for long. Please don't deport him, because we need him every single day.

Rigo's dad was deported four months after he wrote this letter.

Shoot Me Dead
by Yesica. 12 years old. August 2009

My pencil is writing but they're meaningless words
Looking at the teacher but not attentive to what occurs
My thinking somewhere else but here
Thoughts after school are relaxing on beer.

One more friend now vanished and gone
Crossing the border, three shots hit the ground, he was done
Just before his loss, a painful climb
Uncle Peewee shot down, tased four times
His eyes now closed with no second chance
With him now gone, no air to breathe, no song to dance
His eyes now closed, left two kids behind
Border patrol tarred his life, I wish it was mine
Want to plead forgiveness on part of border patrol
Want to help my family and friends overcome anger and take control
Want to retaliate back at border patrol for all the illegals killed
Want to let them know they're creating empty spaces that once were filled
Families got no choice but to fill them up with pictures of the past
Many now realize what they have can be gone
with just three shots or a flash
People risking lives just for their family's need
Innocents dying while there are others creating havoc, smoking weed
The laws just making up lies that create our reputation
Thought this was a free country, not an anti-Mexican nation.

Wanna take a moment of this world's time
To remember all the illegals that have died
I know I'm just twelve and you think I don't understand
Question for border patrol
"How does it feel watching an innocent die with a gun in hand?"

Can they sleep at night knowing there are families dying with tears?
Kids getting angry, ready for revenge, converting into their worst fears
Why kill an illegal when you can just send them back?
What's the point just killing and faking illegals attacked?
When in reality border patrol had fun chasing and shooting them down
But soon their time will come because what goes around comes around
So many innocents blacking out, hitting the cold ground
So many illegals now dead with stories to be found
Point is border patrol likes shooting Mexicans
Can't deny it because it's true
So if I ran with no sign of attack, would you shoot me too?
If you caught me running helpless, what would you do?
Would you fake my attack and shoot me too?
So many harmless people killed, families spread apart
My country is Mexico, border patrol can shoot me, aiming for my heart
People going back to their country still end up shot in the head
I'm not an illegal but if you see me crossing the border
Go ahead
Shoot me dead.

What If They Were One of Us?

by an Anonymous Male Student. 15 years old. February 2010

I think that it is good to have papers because you can go back and forth to visit your mom and family, that's what we would like to do, where we don't have to worry so much about crossing the desert walking. We wish we could go back and forth, to see that place, to see how it looks now, or the family to see what they look like. It has been a long time. I haven't seen them.

If my parents had papers, they would not worry about struggling with finding a job. They have to work nights, evenings, more difficult jobs, it takes them longer to get jobs and some people work where it doesn't pay that good, doesn't give them what they need.

I worry because my parents are working too much and I mostly do not get to see a lot of them at home. I want to spend time with them.

The Americans act normal like me, what is the difference anyway, do you know?

I think the only difference is that the Americans have a lot of money and that's all. They get their kids everything they want, everything new, but for us we only get something if we have money, it depends on the money. And also we have to live together, like crowded, all together. Americans are in better places than us.

But what if they were one of us? Would they enjoy the life we are living or the way we are treated?

Farm Work

"You cannot uneducate the person who has learned to read. You cannot oppress the people who are not afraid anymore. We have seen the future, and the future is ours."

—César Chavez

My Hands Are Colored
by Teresa & Roberto. 14 & 12 years old. January 2011

Meanwhile I am working
Meanwhile I am smiling
I feel tired
My hands are colored
It's really hot
Time don't stop
It's too cold
Nothing to cover
Meanwhile I see myself suffering
I tell myself just keep trying
The children not doing well at school
The teachers think that ain't cool
It's rainy I feel dirty
No matter what happens
I still do it
No matter what people say
Still I need to help my family
I feel tired
My hands are colored.

Suffering in the Fields
Doodle and writing by Roberto. 12 years old. January 2011

I am Roberto. I'm twelve years old. In the summer I work in the fields. I do strawberry, raspberry, blackberry, and sometimes I do blueberry. We in our family are ten, four sisters and four boys. We live in a house.

I was working in the fields and I saw a lot of people working, even little kids. I felt that their parents were suffering. I thought, this is me too, suffering in the fields, getting wet in the morning, hot in the afternoon, going home late.

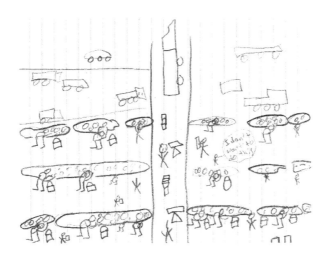

Working in the berry fields.

I Suffer but I'm Proud

Doodle and writing by Frank. 16 years old. January 2011

I remember one time when I was working in the fields and I felt the pain that my parents were feeling working in the field to maintain us. I saw little kids working. Some of them didn't go to summer school because their parents needed them to help in the fields. I work in the fields under the hot sun bending down picking strawberries. Later I start to feel a lot of pain on my back. I suffer; this made me think about my future. I started seeing myself working in the fields all my life if I dropped out of school. Then I said to myself that I'm tired of working in the fields. I prefer going to school and graduating so I could get a better job.

Now I know that being an immigrant ain't something to be ashamed of. Back then when I was a little kid, I was criticized. They called me "Oaxaco". I felt bad. So the day after, or some time, I was going to places with my parents, and I was embarrassed to be with them. But when I was in the 7th grade, everything changed. I started to be proud of my parents' race. I felt like I wanted people to know where my parents are from, just like the Chinese, Japanese, Koreans, and Puerto Ricans are known here in the U.S. So now when people ask me where I work I tell them that I work in the fields picking strawberries, raspberries, pickles (cucumbers), blueberries, and blackberries. Also if some people ask me where my parents are from, I proudly tell them that my parents are from Oaxaca. Also if people ask me what language I speak at home and what language my parents speak, I tell them, "I speak Spanish and English. I also understand a little of my parents' language, Mixtec. My parents speak Mixtec and Spanish."

Working in the Fields
Doodle and writing by Vladimir. 13 years old. January 2011

I was working in the fields and I saw a rabbit and *Arabes* (Arabs). I thought the Arabes might be family of the owners. They talk behind my back. They judge me by making fun of me.

When I saw my parents suffer I felt like I should help and when my dad would carry the berries I would take over and carry them.

My apartment has a window in every room and when I get home I see my sister with her baby and my mom making bread. She is always rather exhausted, sleeping, or tired.

Straddling Two Worlds

by Janice Blackmore. Migrant Graduation Specialist. October 2011

In the classroom, migrant students often do not feel comfortable or successful. They sometimes struggle academically due to language and culture barriers, and frequent moves can cause significant holes in their education. They may feel proud of a good grade, an award, or selection for a special honor, yet often their academic pride is not easily understood at home due to their parents' lack of educational experience in Mexico and/or the U.S.

It is common for migrant students to feel more comfortable and successful in the fields than they do in the classroom. In general, parents of migrant students most value children who work hard and help support the family. Migrant students can tell you how fast they can pick blueberries and exactly how much money they earned for the family over the summer. Unfortunately, the pride the students feel in the fields is not validated in our educational system, nor in our culture as a whole.

Migrant students are forced to straddle these two worlds and, ultimately, they are forced to choose only one.

The Fields Are Better Than School
by Moisés. 12 years old. January 2011

I was working in the fields and I thought it was better working cause being in school is boring and I thought it was better being where you move and don't sit and feel bored like in school. But it is a pain in the ass just to get up to go to work.

When I think about my family, I feel cool in our own way.

I Will Stay in School
by Guadalupe. 14 years old. January 2011

I remember one time when I was working in the fields and I saw a lot of people working. I felt bad because I saw how hard the people worked and they had a bad salary. I thought about how much and how hard our parents work and I learned to appreciate more what they give me. I felt so bad that I decided that I wanted to stay in school because I did not want to end up working like them.

When I am in school I feel good because I see my friends and I have fun with them. I used to not like school because it was boring but now I am starting to like school more and I am also trying to always get good grades and stay on track while I am in school. Mount Baker Middle School is a good school.

When I think about my family I feel sad because I would like it if we all had good communication.

The People

From <u>In My Mother's House</u>, by Ann Nolan Clark
Selected by Alejandro I. 14 years old. September 2011

We are the people
Living together,
All of us together.

We live here
In the houses,
In the plaza
Together.

When it is dark
All of us are sleeping.

When it is day
We are working,
Always
Together.

It is good to stand close
Like our houses.

My Migrant Life
by Teresa. 14 years old. January 2011

Hi, my name is Teresa. I live in a white house and it has three rooms and a restroom. I sleep with my three sisters and I have a T.V. and I have a refrigerator and it has food and drink and I have a table that on top has tortillas. I have a floor with carpet.

In the fields, I saw my parents suffering by picking up heavy boxes and I felt bad so I started working faster on the strawberries and the weather was around 90 degrees. I remember one time when I was working in the fields and I saw a snake and I felt scared and cold and I thought I was going to die.

I remember one time when someone criticized me by telling me I am stupid because I listen when my parents tell me what to do. And I thought about it and I said, "I am not stupid because I know I am doing the right thing," so I went up to her and told her, "At least I have parents with me and at least I have a future."

When I think about my family I feel proud and I feel we are a lot, because some people say that.

Something I never talk about is feelings.

Struggling to Survive
by Eber. 13 years old. September 2011

When they come to the U.S.A.
Many people what they do is pray
To have a good life, to earn some money.
When you're illegal it ain't a joke, it ain't funny.
There are many people who come with a dream.
My people never stop they work as a team.

I worked really hard to come this way.
And I will keep working cause I'm here to stay.
I worked in the fields in the burning sun.
The work is hard and it ain't very fun.
We worked for years just for freedom.
I see my people on their knees and I don't like how they treat 'em.

The president promised us things.
He illuminated our dreams.
His words filled our lives with illusions.
Everything from the start, they were just confusions.

My people are still waiting.
The months and years go by.
We're still working in the sun
We keep waiting and waiting and we're forgetting why.
There are a lot of people.
We come and go from place to place
Some people try to put us down.
But we're still proud of our race.
Some are wanting laws
To get us out of here.
My people keep on struggling
But we walk with no fear.

We keep living our lives
And we keep moving on,
Keep working on our American dream,
But it's taking too long.

Struggles

"Be kind, for everyone you meet is fighting a great battle."

—Plato

Obstacles We Face

Things that could keep me from graduating: doing drugs, gangs, moving to somewhere, or getting tired.

by Moisés. 12 years old. January 2011

Looking ahead, things that could keep me from graduating from high school would be: doing drugs then suddenly I'm addicted to it; getting into trouble at school, then getting expelled; going too deep in the gangs then ending up doing time; killing someone for the gang; parents putting me to work; one of my parents dying so that I'll have to work to help maintain my brothers and sister; or getting a girl pregnant then being forced to marry her.

by Frank. 15 years old. January 2011

Things that could keep me from graduating: bad influences, working, family, getting pregnant, or if someone dies.

by Guadalupe. 14 years old. January 2011

Desperation
by Celia. 15 years old. January 2011

I can't believe that I am fifteen and all that I feel is like my life has changed. I don't know if I am stupid or dumb but I don't understand who I AM. I want to focus in school but it just stops me…I just can't do it. It is too hard to live how I live. There are a lot of things that I want to be, but I feel like I could never ever get there. It is just too hard. When you go through things that are very difficult…you just can't make it where you want to. You think too much about what if that happens again or what if I make a mistake on purpose or what if this or that. I am just not happy.

I feel like quitting no matter what!

Leukemia

Dictated by Vladimir. 14 years old. October 2011

I was four or five when my Aunt Rosa got cancer - leukemia.

My dad was working in the fields and he was *mayordomo* (foreman). We had a two-story house and a one-story house in Oxnard, California. My dad and mom saved up money so that if something happened to them we could rely on that.

When my dad found out his sister was sick, he left us all and went to take care of her and he used all of that money, $50,000, to help her. She was in Tijuana. It cost a lot of money over there, the medicine and all of that. He eventually ran out of money and asked his brothers and sisters if they would help. They said no, but they did loan him money so he could help her himself. My Aunt Rosa wanted to see her sister, Tia Juana, who was living in California, but my Tia Juana didn't want to see her. So my dad convinced her and paid for her to fly to Mexico, paid for her ticket, her expenses, and gave her money. Soon after Tia Juana's visit, my Aunt Rosa died, so my dad came home.

At that time, my other aunt, Tia Carmen, wanted our one-story house because we owed her money too. So my dad let her stay at that house and we stayed in the big house, the two-story house.

Then my mom got a tumor in the stomach. She didn't feel good, so my parents went back to Tijuana and borrowed money to pay for the operation. She had a small tumor but they caught it early enough they were able to take it out. If she'd waited a little bit longer, it could have been a serious problem.

My older brother joined the football team at Oxnard High School. He was good. He only played in one game. A couple days after the game, my mom took him to the hospital and they said he didn't have anything. But my brother still didn't feel good so my mom took him again and they said he had leukemia. My brother expected it because before this he went to church and the priest brought two people in, my brother and another man, and he told them they would both get leukemia – one would die and one would survive. My brother had to go to Los Angeles, an hour away, for the shots and his medication. Since he had no medical insurance, we had to pay for everything.

We couldn't afford the big house any more, so we sold it. My Tia Carmen moved out of the one-story house so we could move in. I was going to start a new school, but then my mom and dad took my two brothers, my sister, and me to Mount Vernon to work in the blueberries. (We left my sick brother and my oldest sister in California.) We stayed with my uncle in Mount Vernon and worked in Lynden. This was during the school year, but we did not go to school. We only worked. I was nine years old.

My dad was in debt $20,000, not to the bank, but to my family members. They let him borrow money instead of helping my Aunt Rosa themselves. My dad gave practically all of the money we earned in the fields to my uncle because we owed him so much money.

On August 15th, I had my tenth birthday in Mount Vernon, and then we went back to California at the end of the month to be with my brother and sister. Eventually we moved the whole family here for better access to health care for my sick brother, Danny.

Ever since then, my dad has been taking my brother, my sister, and me to work in Lynden during the summer to pay off the debt. Last year he finally paid off all of it, but my family is still working hard to have the life that we once had. My mom started her own little business growing, harvesting, and selling the vegetables that she grows. My sister and I help her a lot. I go to school during the day and sometimes help her after school and on the weekends. Now that it's winter, she's not going to need me that much so I get to stay at home.

I think some day we will have as much money as we once had in California.

Oh, and remember the other man at church with leukemia? He died.

These six essays were written in an attempt to win a lap desk designed for migrant students by Janice Blackmore's husband, Daniel Galán.

Where Do I Do My Homework?

In the Bathroom
by Angelina. 15 years old. June 2011

I hope I can get my desk.

W ant it so badly.
A lways doing homework.
N o, definitely the bathroom is not a good place to do
    my work, but it is the only spot I have.
T ell me that I can get it please!

T hat desk will definitely help to do my work.
H ow can I show you I am the right person to choose?
I f I don't get it I will be fine too.
S o I will be waiting to go to high school and continue my education.

D ifferent and more difficult high school is going to be.
E ducation is the only way out of my situation.
S o I'll be positive and wish for that best.
K ind you are, giving up your little desk to a lucky kid.

At Home When No One's There
by Mayra. 13 years old. June 2011

I do not do my homework everyday because when my family goes anywhere I do my homework, but when they are home I do not. There's always noise everywhere and I have my room but I share with her. I can't do my homework on the desk in the kitchen because there are always people and I don't have a desk to work my homework on and I can't stay after school because I have to take care of my little brothers. I want a desk that I can take everywhere with me.

On the Bed I Share with My Brother
by José. 13 years old. June 2011

The place where I do my homework is on my bed. I feel comfortable working there. I like this place because it's very quiet. I have plenty of space to spread out all my papers and see them all at once. But when my brother comes back from work he wants his bed back and I don't have my space anymore. I wish I could have my own room and my own desk.

At Home, But It's Really Hard for Me
by Carolina S. 15 years old. June 2011

H ome, it is really hard for me to do my homework because there is always something cold in me – fear, emptiness.

O utside of my home is hard too. I don't know where to be, life is hard, there are sometimes that it's like the darkness of evil.

M y home reminds me too much of stuff of my past when my birthday was close to come, one day with no strength.

E ven though I try hard in school it can't take me nowhere where I can be free and feel like me, like before.

W hy did life have to bring me something so difficult that I can't handle it sometimes? But it all depends on me, always me.

O ne day at least I want freedom. I want to be somewhere where I'm going to be happy once and for all.

R emembering my past makes me weak like a baby that can barely get up and start walking.

K nowing that there are sometimes challenges in life that you just can't stand, remember I do my best "here".

En la Cocina
(In the Kitchen)
by Exell (winner of the desk). 14 years old. June 2011

Hago mi tarea	I do my homework
En la cocina	In the kitchen
Está un poquito sucia	It's a little dirty because
Porque mi carnal la ensucia	My brother makes a mess
Luego no me puedo concentrar	Later I can't concentrate
Porque él hace mucho ruido	Because he's so noisy
Y luego me está	And later he's bugging me
Molestando	Or if not that
O si no	He's yelling
Está gritando	Later he starts to run around
Luego empieza a correr	Later his friends come over
Luego llegan sus amigos	And they make all sorts of noise
Y hacen un escandalo como	Like playing music or if not that
Ponen música o si no	They're whining
Están llorando	But I try and I do a little
Pero trato y hago poquita	Homework and the rest
Tarea y la demás	I do it in school in the morning
Yo la hago en la	With help from the teachers
Escuela en la mañana	Later I turn it in
Con ayuda de los maestros	And they give me
Luego la entrego	A good grade for my class.
Y me dan	
Una buena calificacion en la clase.	

In My Crazy House
by Roberto. 13 years old. June 2011

I'm sitting on my bed with my three brothers, my mom making food, my little sister crying for her bottle, my sister screaming. I can't concentrate. I go get a drink when I come back my brother tells me to move because he's going to work out. I go to the living room, on the couch my sister and brother are watching Sponge Bob, running around the house going outside then coming back, my mom yelling at them, if you're going to stay in the house stay, if you're not then get out. I CAN'T THINK NO MORE.

My Life is Difficult
Painting and writing by Celia. 14 years old. October 2010

At 5:00am I woke up and started thinking, why is my life so difficult?
I just feel like I am never liked from wherever I am at. I think about quitting school but halfway through I think about my teachers of what they say to me to never quit (school) so I could have a better job and more money, that is Mrs. Blackmore and Mrs. Goodrich. I don't know what to do for them or what to give them because they make me feel like they were my family who cares about me.

6:20am I started getting ready for my school, thought I would feel better but it was worse. Then about 8:20am or 8:30am I talked to Mrs. Solís about my feelings of how I'm hurt and why.

7:30pm – 8:20pm My life is difficult, especially when I'm with my family because there are times that they are mean to me. My life is like being on a street that sometimes goes nowhere because my feelings get hurt too much. School and home don't make me happy too much. In school it is hard especially when I don't talk to anybody. I like to work by myself but sometimes they say I don't have friends and I don't have anybody to talk to.

I like to be friendly to everyone but there are times people make me mad and I even say things back too. I never insult someone for who they are or where they're from. There are sometimes they insult me but I don't do it back. The reason why is because I know how it feels to be insulted.

A speech to school staff, written by a member of the Migrant Leaders Club.

No More Judgement
by Rosie. 14 years old. October 2011

Hi, my name is Rosie, for those of you who don't know me. I came here to talk to you about how the Migrant Leaders Club wants to make a change here at LaVenture Middle School.

We want to change the culture in the school so there is no judgment of others.

We migrant students chose to work on judgment because some of us have experience with disrespect and disgrace at LaVenture. Sometimes kids make fun of us because of how we look or where we're from. Those names that I hear when I walk down the LaVenture halls make me feel worth nothing.

However, it's not just migrant students. Every culture is sometimes disrespected and disgraced at LaVenture. I'm saying all this because I have seen all kinds of people getting disrespected and disgraced by others that just don't know how they feel inside when they're called names as if they're worth nothing. I feel like I kind of know how they feel. My thinking is, "why are those people doing that to people that they don't even know?" I think they just want to do that for fun because they want to be popular.

For you to understand better, because I want you to understand what I'm trying to say, let me explain that I have seen people get called names, for example Oaxaquito, Oaxaca fresh, etc. Those names can be an offense to others. I know that the majority of Oaxacans get mad and they defend themselves when they're called those names. I know that they shouldn't fight, that the right thing is that they should just tell one of the teachers so they can help them out with their problem. I know that I would want to do that instead of getting in trouble and getting the blame for what I haven't started. I would like to talk to all students bout this change we want to see, not just the students who are judging but all students because we can work together.

I have a question. How would you feel if you were a migrant student or someone that gets bullied all the time because of how you look and where you're from? I know for a fact that nobody wants to be disrespected or feel disgraced. My goal is that I want all this judgment to stop at once at

LaVenture so nobody will feel this way again. Judgment makes people feel like this school is not going to be safe for people that want a good education for themselves.

I would like to invite you teachers to help us with our project so this judgment will stop happening at LaVenture. I want to give you some examples of how you can help:

1.   Be a good role model to the students and don't judge. I'm not saying that you do, but just be a good role model.

2.   Feel comfortable and safe asking us questions about how we feel about our culture, about the judgment we are seeing at LaVenture, and if we are getting judged and how we feel about that.

3.   Talk to your classes about our project and invite them to help us stop the judgment at LaVenture.

Thank you for listening to what I had to say today. I said all of this because I want you to know what we have seen and how we feel about judgment at LaVenture. We think we can make a change if we all work together.

Theater of the Oppressed

Last year we practiced Paulo Freire's Theater of the Oppressed one day per week as a way for migrant students to explore different experiences with oppression and how they might create change in their school and in their lives. Based on that work, the ESL language arts class decided to write scripts on actual moments when they felt disrespected at school. Other individual students wrote scripts about struggles outside of school. These scripts were then acted out, changed, and changed again as students explored alternate actions and reactions.

Theater of the Oppressed Scripts - In School
by LaVenture Middle School ESL Language Arts Class. June 2011

Setting: Student is walking to Ms. Goodrich's room with lunch when a staff member stops her.

Staff:	"Where are you going?"
Student:	"I'm going to Ms. Goodrich's class."
Staff:	"You can't go there with your lunch!"
Student:	"But Ms. Goodrich lets us."
Staff:	"I don't care! There are ants getting in the classes because of that!"

Staff walks away a little mad.

Student walks to Ms. Goodrich's, mad.

Student starts eating her lunch in Ms. Goodrich's class, uncomfortable because of staff.

Staff comes to Ms. Goodrich's classroom and sees the student eating.

Staff:	"I told you not to come here!"
Student:	Says mad things quietly...

Setting: Two students are walking down the hall chatting.

Student 1:	*"Oye, que vas a hacer esta fin de semana?"*
Student 2:	*"Mira dude, no sé ..."*
Teacher :	(Interrupting) "None of that! We speak English here."
Student 1:	"Whatevers, dude."
Student 2:	Laughs and slaps friend's back. Students walk off laughing.

Setting: Some students are hanging out waiting for a teacher in a hallway outside a classroom.

Teacher:	Approaches aggressively, angry look on face. "What are you guys doing in the hallway?"
Student:	Squares shoulders, angry look on face. "We're waiting for our teacher."
Teacher:	"You know you're not supposed to be hanging out in the hall. Go wait in the cafeteria. Go on!" Shoos students like dogs.

Students slowly turn and start to walk away

Student::	Angrily says mad things quietly.
Teacher:	(Angry) "What did you say?"
Student:	(Angry) "Nothing! None of your business!"
Teacher:	"What's your name? You're getting a poor choice slip!"
Student:	"I don't care!"

Setting: A parking lot outside a middle school during a fire drill. Three students are bouncing a tree branch up and down shaking the pollen off of the tree. A teacher comes up to the students.

Teacher 1:	"Hey, what are you guys doing? Stop shaking that tree. You know that can get in your eyes and affect you. Some people are allergic to it and you might not know it. Move away from there. Go on. Move."

The three students move away. One student who was standing near them stays where he is.

Teacher 1:	"I said move. Come on, let's go."
Student:	"But I wasn't doing anything. Why do I have to move? Damn."
Teacher:	"What's your name?"
Student:	"Gerardo."
Teacher 2:	Approaches and addresses Teacher 1. "Maybe you and Gerardo can go somewhere else and talk."
Teacher 1:	"No, I think we're done." Walks away.

Theater of the Oppressed Scripts - At Home (Fiction)
by Tina. 14 years old. February 2011

Dad: Kids, behave, we're leaving.
Mom: Clean the house. I already made food so you guys could eat.
Jenny: Okay mom.

Parents leave.

Rafael: Get up and let's go.
Carlos: Alright then.
Rafael: Alright.
Omar: Go where?
Rafael: Just come on, hurry up.
Mayra: (Finishes dressing up for a party.)

The boys all leave.

Mayra: Jenny, lock the door.
Jenny: Don't leave me again. (Wanting to cry.)

Mayra's Boyfriend beeps his horn outside.

Mayra: Bye, my ride is here.

Mayra leaves.

The four brothers are kicking it with friends.
A gang member does a drive by where the boys are at.

Rafael: They're coming – RUN!!

He gets shot because he was Mexican and for the way he was dressed.
He dies.

The next morning-

Dad: Hey kids, wake up, where's Rafael?
Carlos: Oh he stayed at his friend's house.
Mom: Where's Mayra?
Omar: In her room.

Mom opens Mayra's bedroom door.

Mayra: Leave me alone. (She has a bad headache.)
Mom: Why'd you leave your sister alone?
Mayra: Close my door!

Mom closes the door.

Mayra: (to herself) I am NOT going to school today.

Later that day-

Carlos: Let's make a plan.
Alex: What? Revenge?
Omar: I don't want to be in this!
Carlos: Come on, let's do this for our carnal.
Omar: Okay I'll do it.

The three brothers go to kill the people who killed their brother.
The three brothers end up in jail.

Mayra's boyfriend: (drunk) Give me everything you have.
Mayra: Take me to my house!

Mayra and her boyfriend are in a car accident.

The next morning-

Jenny: (Unable to focus.) Bye mom, I am leaving for school.

Police officer knocks on the door

Mom: Hello, who are you looking for?
Officer: Rafael's parents.
Mom: Yes, I am his mom, why?
Officer: Your son has been killed.
Mom: (Crying.) Ooooh no!
Officer: Are you also the parents of Carlos, Alex, and Omar?
Dad: Yes
Officer: They have been sent to jail for a killing.
Dad: For how long?
Officer: For life.

Jenny sits crying in the corner.

Theater of the Oppressed Scripts - On the Bus
Monserrat. 14 years old. January 2011

I remember one time that I was sitting down on the bus and a teacher I didn't know walked up to me and she asked me,

"Hey, you're a beaner, right?"

I just looked at her and told her,

"Well I could be one, but you wouldn't like me to call you a nigga', right? So don't judge a book by its cover."

She gave me a killer look and opened her mouth,

"You...you...bitch! How dare you, insignificant child!"

I felt as if anger and rage ran through my body as a dog with rabies. I thought,

"If I say anything I will be the one that gets in trouble."

I got up from the soft, leather seats of the bus and left.

Monse (back row, middle) at her going-away party before moving to Mexico.

There are a lot of people that hate Mexican people,
a lot of people in the world.

by Celia. 15 years old. February 2011

Tina wrote this letter to fellow students in an attempt to steer them away from gang life.

Bad Girls
by Tina. 14 years old. June 2011

Dear students,

Do you want to get hurt? People, read this letter and you will see what would happen if you're in a gang or want to be in one. Have you ever seen something scary that could have been worse, especially if it happened around your block? So read this letter if you want to know what happened to me.

OK, I barely came from school and I was so hungry and in my house there's a big window in front of the kitchen table and it was so hot that day so I opened it. First I went to the refrigerator and grabbed some fried chicken to eat and like always at my house you have to eat at the table, it's a rule. There was nobody at my house so I kept looking out the window to see if I could find my sister. Then I saw my cousin's girlfriend's teenage sister sitting outside with her dog.

Suddenly a black Cadillac came with a bunch of girls. I felt like it was no big deal. I thought it was just her homegirls. But when I looked carefully, they were yelling at her and saying really, but really bad words. I was watching in the window and seeing and hearing everything that was happening. I didn't know what to do. I felt like I wanted to do something about it because she's family and it was located on my street, but I was afraid that the fight was going to get worse. The good thing was that my older gangster cousin wasn't there because he was at work.

Like twenty minutes later a white car came and joined the bad girls. Inside this white car they were all boys and they were all deep in red. They were bumping up gang music and throwing gang signs. And like I told you, my cousin's girlfriend's sister was still alone with her dog.

My sister came home and I told her to go to the park down the street to get my cousins and my brother to come and help my cousin's girlfriend's sister. While she was gone, I noticed a man next to one of the cars talking on a cell phone. Suddenly the black Cadillac and the white car turned on their engines and drove away fast. Right away the cops showed up asking questions. I don't know who called them.

When the cops left all my cousins and my brother came by and they were standing all around my cousin's girlfriend's sister's house and again minutes passed. The people from the cars came again but walking this time and this time my cousin's girlfriend's sister fought one of the girls. Then another tall woman got in the fight. All my boy cousins were watching but didn't do anything because it was a "girls fight", but they were there in case the other men got in it, which is called "back up".

At that time my heart felt so terrible, like as if it was jumping hard, because she was fighting three girls at the same time. And the other girls were trying to cheat because the boys told them to put rings on their fingers. But the cops were so dumb because they didn't do anything. They just kept coming back every thirty minutes and checking around the block.

In conclusion, this experience helps me understand that it is not good trying to be or being in the gang because you never know if you are going to be by yourself and get beat up by your "enemies".

Your friend,

Tina

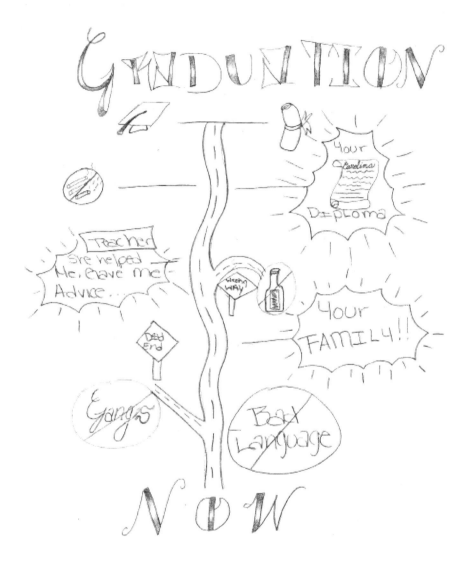

Path to Graduation
by Carolina G. 14 years old. March 2009

Choices

by Yesica. 14 years old. December 2011

This world has its good and bad, fall in love or fall in hate,
Its all your choice, the rest is fate,
Have no worries or be filled with stress,
Have your shyt straight or create a mess,
Be caring or don't care at all,
Don't trip cause then you'll fall,
Keep your head up or keep it down,
Keep a smile and loose a frown,
Start a relationship or put it to an end,
Lose a fake, earn a friend,
Forget the color or begin a war,
Find true love or date a whore,
Speak the truth or forever lie,
Find reasons to keep living or find reasons to die,
Be respectful or always disrespect,
Keep rejecting or learn to accept,
Be true to him/her or just cheat,
Follow your mind or follow your heartbeat,
Live in a home or live in the street,
Give up or be strong and remain on your feet,
Shed some tears or enjoy some laughter,
Be miserable or live happily ever after.

Night Clamming

by Emily Martin. Community Member & Mixtec Advocate. June 2011

Author's Dedication:
I dedicate this to Serapia, Lao, and Elena. For their love, their guidance, and their commitment to me. They have fed me, taught me, counseled me, wiped away my tears and always know how to make me laugh. I dedicate this to them and to all of the other Mixtec families of Skagit who have welcomed me, a stranger. *Xindá'vi iní-ndo, maní ní yu'u nuú-ndo.* (Thank you guys so much, you are true friends.)

The sun was hovering on the horizon when we got off the boat that day. Though we had left in the early afternoon, we had waited nearly an hour for the tide to go out far enough to expose the mud flats. It was evening now but we would work fast with the remaining daylight.

Perhaps it's better to say that they would work fast. I was probably the only one on the boat that day to have any faith in my ability to work. I had already shown that I couldn't start a fire or catch *tioli* (crabs) to boil and eat, or even follow simple instructions.

The directions were quite simple, really. Select a spot, crouch down, press the rake into the mud three times - making the sides and top of a square. Press the rake in at the top and pull back, lifting out a cubic foot of sand. Grab all of the clams in the hole first, before they escape, and then the clams in the mud at your feet.

My first time I fell backwards with the weight of the mud, trapping my foot, flailing on the sand. My second time I grabbed twelve or fifteen clams before I lost my footing and fell forward into the hole. I was cold, wet, and my ego bruised.

I followed Lao and Serapia, dragging my box behind me, learning to balance my weight and dig quickly. I fell less and gathered more each time. I began to fill my box.

By the time my box was three-quarters full I was having trouble carrying it. Lao piled it on top of his own full boxes to carry back. We were now using our headlamps as dusk settled in.

For a time I followed Elena, crouching beside her and grabbing clams out of the cold, muddy water. We worked in silence, having long ago run out of my limited Mixtec vocabulary. Or maybe because under such conditions there is little left to be said between a white and a Mixtec.

Clam diggers earn $0.27 per pound of clams. They suffer from tendinitis and chronic inflammation of the hands and arms.

It's the loneliest feeling under those stars at night but so beautiful I paused for a minute. With my headlamp off, I stood and gazed at the constellations. I could see the lights on the distant shore, cities all around.
I turned to head back. I was there to work after all, to dig clams as they do. They were gone. Nothing left but a muddy hole filling with water.

No footprints, all signs of them washed away. I looked up again. I'd orient myself by the stars or those city lights out on the shore. We came from... well, we left the boat... my headlamp showed me nothing. No boat, no people, just grey sand out to a black horizon. Just me.

I had dressed for the cold, wearing layers like they told me, but I was tired and began to feel chilled. I picked a direction and started walking, fighting back tears.

Later that night, on the boat, we'd laugh about all this. After the men had lifted me on board; after the women had stripped me of my wet clothes and dressed me in their own warm coats. We laughed about how scared I'd been, if only I could've seen my face! they told me. They told me stories of times they'd been afraid, of storms coming through. Sleet and ice. The waves tossing the boat so hard the boxes of clams fell overboard. Going home at night exhausted with not a penny to show for it.

It took us over an hour to return to the dock. The boats are not outfitted with lights or depth finders. There is no map of the channels out there. We frequently ran aground, the engine choked with sand. We ran out of firewood. It began to rain.

I never went back out on that boat, but they do every day, sometimes working two weeks without a day of rest. They haven't forgotten my attempt at solidarity - my one day of work with them. I don't forget that they are out there right now, as I write this, and as you read it.

This is My Voice (Excerpts)
by Shane Koyczan and the Short Story Long
Selected by Thalía. 14 years old. January 2012

This is my voice, there are many like it, but this one is mine...

You see too many live in countries where it's bullets instead of ballots,
where gavels fall like mallets
when held in the hands of those whose judgments can be bought
as easily as children can be taught
to covet,
and the only ones willing to speak up are forced to live so far beneath the
radar that the underground is considered above it...

This is my voice, there are many like it, but this one is mine.

We're not always right,
but we've got the right to be wrong.
We're not always free,
so this is just a short story long.

And this time it's for the sons and daughters
who watch their mothers and fathers
drown in shallow waters
While panning for the "American dream"
in the polluted creek called the mainstream.
This is for the homeless people sleeping on steam vents,
making makeshift tents
out of cardboard and old trash,
trying to catch 40 winks in between the crash
of car wrecks,
risking their necks
by surviving another day so that they can starve,
so that famine can carve
their body into a corpse before their heart stops beating,
so that men in a boardroom meeting
can make it harder for them to get welfare,
health care,
it's no wonder some of them pawn off their own wheelchair,
and every time I walk 'em by, I can't help but feel at fault,
that maybe I didn't search myself hard enough
for the control alt "s"
so that I could SAVE THE WORLD.

Or at least this little girl curled up into a ball.
I've spent most of my life throwing compassion back
like a fish that's too small.
Gotta cash in my reality checks, drop her some spare fantasies
cause I've got three separate degrees
from different universities,
but the most valuable thing I ever learned was to believe people when they
say "PLEASE."

This is my voice, there are many like it, but this one is mine.

We're not always right,
but we've got the right to be wrong.
We're not always free,
so this is just a short story long.

You ever been reeled in, reeled out, picked on, put down, ever been around
to hear the sound when your own heart breaks, start to take the time to take
the time, ever been seen and not heard, you ever blurred the lines for those
who tried to find some way to define what you are, as if you were far from
them, at least at the heart of them, it's more than a part of them. You ever
been told you're too young or too old, well they sold us that line that we're
willing to buy, and we got to receive and then beat the deadlines. So don't try
to define us cause this time we're fine…We're pissed off and loud and now
you know why.

We're not always right,
but we've got the right to be wrong.
We're not always free,
so this is just a short story long…

Tell the world:
"This is my voice, there are many like it, but this one is mine."

The following is an essay submitted to the Association of Farmworker Opportunity Programs' Migrant and Seasonal Farmworker Children Essay Contest. Elissa won second place in this national competition and received $200.

Like a Caged Bird
Elissa. 13 years old. July 2010

My name is Elissa. I'm thirteen years old. I have two little brothers, one older half brother, and one sister. My dad suffered a knee injury and can't work but that doesn't stop him from learning English so he can help me and my siblings on our homework. My mom works very hard ever since she was very young. Two years ago, she got surgery and a few weeks later she started working again in the fields.

My most important dream is to become an actress for Hollywood. My back-up plan is to be a persuasive speaker. My experience of working in the fields will affect my dream because I won't be able to go to drama classes, play practice, or anything that I'm trying to do to achieve my dream of becoming an actress.

I was born in Baja California and from there my family and relatives moved to Madera, California. My uncle was almost a teenager and he took care of me while my mom was working hard. I know how hard my mom suffered giving birth to me because it was a natural birth. From Madera, we moved to Mount Vernon, Washington, and I grew up there.

My dad is an inspiration in my life because he is going to classes to learn English because he never had a dad to force him to go to school. That tells me to go to school because this is a chance for me to get an education and make my dreams come true. My dad grew up poor and so did my mom. I'm going to school and I think it's boring but I have to because this is my chance. Also, my best friend Aracely is an inspiration in my life right now. She has straight A's. I have bad grades. She is inspiring me to get straight A's.

The challenges I'm facing are people and relatives thinking that I'm going to end up like them, working in the fields. Also, my religion: being a Jehovah's Witness for me is like living my life like a caged bird, not free. It's stopping me from being myself and not able to dress how I want and also I have to leave my friends for my religion. I know it's going to be hard for me.

In order to achieve my important dream to follow my dream even though I'm struggling with my weight, religion, and people, I will have to move on and hear the people that believe that I'm going to become an actress. I will take drama classes, audition in plays at school or the theatres where I live. I will also believe in myself and I won't let nobody's words stop me from making my dreams come true. Also, my mom speaks Mixtec and I would love to learn Mixtec so I can translate for those that don't speak Mixtec. It's worth it.

I can accomplish my dream. All I have to do is believe in myself.

Domestic Violence

I strongly support the client's application for asylum. If she returns to Mexico, she will be found by her abusers and there will be no protection available to her; she and her eleven year old daughter will be harmed and may not survive.

My name is Janice Blackmore and I am the Migrant Graduation Specialist for the Mount Vernon School District. I lived in Oaxaca, Mexico, for three years where I worked with young women from indigenous villages. Upon returning to the U.S., I began working with migrant students at LaVenture Middle School, where ten percent of the school's population is Mixtec, an indigenous group from the states of Oaxaca and Guerrero, Mexico. I met my husband while living in Oaxaca and we are raising our daughter bilingually and biculturally. We spend every summer in Oaxaca with my husband's family.

In my opinion, the client cannot safely return to Mexico.

The client comes from the Mixtec region of Mexico, a mountainous area made up of many small villages surrounding three somewhat larger cities. This is one of the poorest and most isolated parts of Mexico. It has remained very much separate from the rest of the country in language, culture, and laws. Mixtec is the official language, although there are so many variations ("dialects") of Mixtec that often the people from two neighboring villages cannot communicate at all. Village traditions date back to before the Spanish conquest. The region's extreme isolation is due to their intentional avoidance of mixing with the "Spanish" culture known throughout the rest of Mexico.

The laws of Mexico do not apply in the Mixtec region. The villages rule by village law and the elders of the villages make the laws. The inter-village fighting that the client references in her declaration dates back hundreds of years. Many members of the Mixtec community here in Northwest Washington have fled Mexico due to the kidnappings and killings that are frequent and unpunished in this area. Due largely to this lack of punishment, domestic violence is an epidemic in the region. Women are considered the property of their men and, thus, domestic violence against women is not seen as a crime. Therefore women have nowhere to go for help. Talking about domestic violence is considered taboo. Women who attempt to leave the Mixtec region to escape domestic violence or threats of death face grave repercussions – they are ostracized from the village, enslaved, or killed.

The social structure of Mixtec villages is very tight and inter-connected. They depend on each other for everything due to their isolation. Generally they are distrustful of people who do not come from their own village. As migration outside of the Mixtec region becomes more common due to economic necessity or fear, the inter-connectedness of the village social structure follows the migrants. In general, this is a positive support to the members of the village living elsewhere. However, in the client's case, this tight-knit social structure makes it nearly impossible for her to hide within Mexico. She relies on the people of her village because she cannot trust outsiders, and yet the same people who support her will, in the end, allow her to be found.

Her distrust of outsiders within Mexico is very valid. The discrimination against indigenous people in Mexico is beyond words. I find it quite frightening. If the client were to try to completely disconnect from her Mixtec community and relocate within Mexico in an attempt to hide from her abusers, she would certainly not be able to provide for her daughter and herself. Without an already-established family member or friend from the village, the client would find it impossible to reestablish herself in a city outside of the Mixtec region. Centuries of discrimination would stop her in her tracks. She would find herself begging in the streets, where she would be subject to even more abuse. The client knows no one in Mexico that is not from her village. There is no safe place for her in Mexico.

I would like to include here just a sampling of the plethora of information available about the high rates of domestic violence in the Mixtec and why women do not look for help.

In an article about the high rate of "feminicidios", or the killing of women, in the Mixtec, they suggest that 88% of indigenous women in the Mixtec are victims of abuse.
http://www.noticiasnet.mx/portal/principal/repuntan-feminicidios-mixteca-5-muertas-2-meses

While noting that the Mixtec region ranks first place in cases of violence against women in Oaxaca, the president of the Oaxacan Center for Human Rights and Consultancy for Indigenous Villages states that he believes the cause lays in the complete lack of protection for women or consequences for their abusers: "It's worth nothing that governmental impunity and complacency…makes the killing of women possible, not only in the Mixtec region, but throughout the country.". (my translation)
http://webcache.googleusercontent.com/search?q=cache:hI1dGn3IcnoJ:www.dia-riodelamixteca.com/mixteca/la-mixteca-primer-lugar-en-violencia-contra-la-mujer.html+&cd=3&hl=en&ct=clnk&gl=us

Although I find it to be quite discriminatory and condescending, I would like to include an article titled, "Tlaxiaco is First Place in Killing of Women", because they talk specifically about the municipality of Tlaxiaco, from which the client fled, and its extreme rates of domestic violence: "…98 percent of women are violated in different ways, but the majority don't report it out of fear, which is attributed to their lack of culture, particularly when they are not employed and think that, without the man, they can not support their children." (my translation)

http://www.oaxaca-ya.com/index.php?option=com_content&view=article&id=8367%3Atl axiaco-es-primer-sitio-en-feminicidios&catid=37%3Aal-minuto&Itemid=1

I believe that after reading the above descriptions of life for women in the Mixtec region of Mexico, it should be evident why the client did not immediately look for help upon her arrival in the United States.

- She had never in her life received help or protection of any kind – <u>not once</u>.
- Living in Lynden, WA., so close to the U.S./Canadian border, she was terrified of the police and border patrol who, as she mentions, work closely together. She certainly couldn't turn to them for help.
- The client found herself completely isolated and with a deep distrust of everyone around her. Her only contact with others was at work, where she was surrounded by "untrustworthy" non-Mixtec Mexicans who spoke Spanish, the client's second language.
- Perhaps most importantly, the client was raised to believe that her abuse was normal. She did not see herself as a victim or deserving of help. It simply did not occur to her.

The client won her case and was granted asylum in the U.S.

My Life is like an Apple Cut in Half
by Elizabeth S. 14 years old. March 2008

If you knew me you would know that my life is like an apple cut in half. The first half of my apple is my life at home. Why do I need to do everything: clean, wash dishes, study, do homework? Can I just have a break? I know I am the only girl in my family, but why can't I just concentrate on the other half of my apple – school? I don't understand how I get all A's in my classes when I have so many other things to do. You might think that I am an ordinary girl like others in school and that I just concentrate on one thing, but not everyone is like that. Some people just think about themselves and not about others. I am not like that.

Illegal Love
Elizabeth R. 17 years old. April 2011

I didn't know I'd end up like this. My life has been really difficult since I finished elementary school. My dream was to go to middle school then to high school, but I let my dream go. I never made it to middle school. I know it is not too late, but… Right now I'm having a hard time.

When I was fourteen I got together with my boyfriend and we had a baby. Unfortunately it wasn't good because we got into problems with the authorities of Mount Vernon because I was too young to have a baby with a boy that was six years older than me. Under the law, it is called "rape" because I'm a child and he is an adult, but that's how we do it in our Mixtec culture. That's how we are, but the people in the United States don't seem to understand us.

There was not much problem when I had my baby boy. They just told us that we couldn't have another baby for three years and we said, "OK, no problem", but I often couldn't take birth control and guess what happened? I ended up pregnant again and right away I remembered that they said no more kids or else they would put my boyfriend in jail.

On the morning of December 9th, my boyfriend went with me to the birthing room. I was really worried that they might take him to jail. I was also worried because I had a C-section with my first child and I was hoping not to have one again. When my little girl was born that day I did have the C-section again, because I am diabetic.

Just after the C-section, the police came into the room where I was recovering with my baby and my boyfriend. One of the police men said, "We've come to take your boyfriend and if you would please sign your name here." I wrote my name and I felt… really, how can I explain it to you? sad, hopeless, depressed, mad. I just looked at my baby with tears in my eyes. This was the worst thing that had ever happened to me. I didn't feel good that day in the hospital and I ended up with a fever. This all happened in the same day, the day that I gave birth. I was sixteen.

I went to live with my mom and after two months my boyfriend came to see the kids and to see me because we missed each other. We have been together for so long that for us we are already a family, even though we are not a family to the authorities.

A couple of days passed and at ten o'clock at night the sheriff police came banging on the door and looking for my boyfriend to take him to jail. Luckily my brother was in the living room. He opened the door. "We are looking for this guy and we're going to take him with us," they said. My brother told them, "He's not here; he's with his mom at the store." Then the police said, "If we find that he is here, you are going to be arrested for hiding him." My brother really did think he was at the store, but he wasn't. He was in the bedroom. A couple of minutes later the police found him outside after he jumped out a window. Then they came knocking on the door again. My brother opened the door and the sheriff police said, "Put your shoes on, you're coming with us." So as my brother put his shoes on, I went up to the policeman and I asked him, "Why are you taking my brother? He didn't know my boyfriend was here." I got so mad and then the cop said to me, "I'm not taking him anywhere!" He got mad too and he yelled at me.

Eventually we had to pay a bail bond to get my boyfriend out of jail.
Today they still don't want us together because I'm not eighteen yet. I can't see him and he can't see the kids. My kids think that my big brother is their dad because he's at home with us and they always see him.

So I'm guessing that the courtroom and the police station should be really happy, separating the children from their father and the girlfriend from her boyfriend. Those people have nothing to worry about because they have a family, unlike some people from other cultures who are suffering right now from not being allowed to be together like a family, not allowed to celebrate together, not allowed to have family fun.

They don't want my boyfriend and me to be together just because I'm seventeen. I don't really know if we're every going to be a family. To be a family is very good, very nice because it's all about love. The word FAMILY means a lot of things to me, for example together, happy, love, helping each other, watching over each other. Family is a beautiful word, but some people just don't understand. It looks as if they are selfish, just wanting their own happiness, not caring about other people's feelings, not caring about what others want or what they like.

I hope whoever reads this understands me and tries at least for a minute to put themselves in my situation. If you do, you will understand that this is not a fair situation for any human, because that is who we are – humans with feelings, humans who hurt. I really hope you all understand.

My Obstacles and Dreams
by Alejandro R. 14 years old. November 2011

When I was six years old, my dad drove me across the U.S./Mexico border with my brothers, Victor and Ruben. My dad told me that we were going to get something to eat.

They dressed my brother as a girl because his birthday was the same as another girl that had papers.

My mom had to walk across the border because we didn't have papers for her.

In my life, we moved around three times. The first time I moved was from Mexico to California. When I moved to California, I had to go to school. I did not understand anything. I was about six or seven years old. It was hard to learn English, but later I kind of learned English.

What I do over the summer is go to work with my dad and my two little brothers. We work in the blueberries all the way in Lynden and Sumas. Before the blueberries start, I go with my mom to work in the strawberries. It's hard to work in the fields. You get tired fast but you have to work hard to get money. Sometimes it's raining, or it's really hot. Sometimes you just want to go home.

An obstacle in my life is school. I would like to finish school to have a good job someday. School has been hard for me because of language.

Language has been an obstacle for me. It has been hard to learn English. Sometimes I don't understand what the teacher says; sometimes I don't know what we're doing in class.

My dream is to succeed at school. I would like to be an FBI investigator someday. To accomplish that goal, I think I will need to finish high school and go to college. I hope I can do it.

illustration by Eber. 14 years old. October 2011

Realizations

"Shoot for the moon.
Even if you miss, you'll land among the stars."

—Les Brown

Elizabeth submitted the following college admissions essay to Western Washington University, University of Washington, and Central Washington University and was accepted at all three. She is still undecided about where she will study in the fall.

Responsibility
by Elizabeth S. 18 years old. December 2011

As I got home from school, I saw suitcases running against the wall. My heart started to beat three times harder than regular, because I knew what was coming.

There I stood at my front door waving at my parents, while in my head things were spinning. There were multiple feelings that ran through me. There was fear and frustration, fear of failing this journey I was about to take, frustration toward my parents for leaving me in charge of our house.

My parents went to Mexico for an emergency and I had to stay in Mount Vernon because of school. The reason my brother and I stayed was to not miss school as we did when we went to Mexico a couple years ago.

It wasn't easy being away from my parents for a long time. My life totally turned around from a girl that depended on her parents, to a girl that had to deal with all of the responsibilities that a home requires. I have worked before but it was during the summer with my parents. This time, I was on my own. There was no one to tell to go pay the rent and bills. On the first week of every month you would see me sitting on the couch counting my money and dividing the money for the rent and the electricity bill. I had to make sure to pay them on time.

I struggled going to school and working to have money to pay all of the bills and other house expenses that I had to pay, like laundry detergent and money to go do the laundry. I noticed my grades were dropping which was even more load on me. My grades have always been my priority. I wasn't willing to accept that my grades were going down. Instead I took advantage of every minute I had to go for help on homework I didn't understand before I had to head for work. As days went by I learned to manage my time. I took every minute of my breakfast and lunch to do homework that I didn't have time to do the night before. By the end of my workday, I would go home, hoping for some rest but I had to cook for my brother, clean, and do homework. I couldn't even lie on the couch because I would fall asleep and would get no homework done. At work I was exhausted with no strength or energy;

I didn't even feel like talking or starting a conversation. Only when I went to sleep was there relief from the load that was on me. As days went by it got closer to the date my parents were coming back, which gave me strength to keep going.

My parents were gone for five months. Because they were gone so long my days turned into daily routines.

Now that I look back I see that this experience has been the most rewarding experience that I have gone through. I learned to be on my own, manage my time wisely, and, the most important, responsibility. Even though I had my ups and downs from this experience, it stepped me into the real life I would face in college. As some said, I grew out of my baby clothes.

You See Me As Trouble
by Janet. 14 years old. February 2010

You see me as trouble, mean, not good enough, but you don't see what's underneath me.

You'll see a girl who has gone through humiliation and struggles,

A girl who wants something better than what she seems to be worth,

A girl who knows the understanding of leadership and justice, to dream big, and to never give up,

A girl who is willing to do anything to succeed,

A girl who dreams, respects, and works hard to deserve dreams and make them become reality.

I have the ability and strength to educate myself to overcome my challenges, to become stronger,

I have the freedom to raise myself and to stand tall and strong.

I shine without light.

There isn't another person who is as well-educated as me.

I am Janet and I am proud of myself.

Learner

Shannon Saylor. Teacher. LaVenture Middle School. November 2009

There's a moment of recognition on your face, you light up
Like you possess all knowledge of the world
Like you are the most lucky,
Most joyful,
Most blessed
To have now understood.

It might as well have been the secret to life, but it was just
One word—pizzazz, summon, murder, just words
Encountered in a seemingly trivial task.
Read this story, write this summary.
For you, a battle to the end, you or the word, raging
Unnoticed in the midst of a 7th grade class.
You reach your finger out and place it on the letters, sizing up the word.
The dramatic world of the middle school swooshes
Past you, still, quiet, wrestling with a word. And brave enough
To look into my face, your soul peeking out at mine, and ask me
"What does this mean?"

Alma (on left) and friends

Mi Futuro
(My Future)
by Alma. 14 years old. August 2009

Take a look at me
Tell me what you see
Do you see my smile
That someday will go miles?
Five to ten years I'll be a mother
Work as an actress, or other
Live in a four-story house
And be a happy spouse
I'll have a loving husband
Who will love me to the end
I'll be a woman that loves with her heart
And probably silly and smart
I'm not going to be the girl my mom holds dear
I'll be a lady that has no fear
I'll be the one to look you in the eye
And say "You said I couldn't touch the sky"
I'll do it all and more
For the one I adore
But now I'm all you see
Just a girl that truly believes.

Estoy Aqui!

(Here I Am!)

by Cilviana. 14 years old. September 2011

I am determined.

My mom would describe me as her
princesa
My friends call me scandalous.

I keep dreaming
I remember tears
I've learned to never give up
I hide sadness
I read faces.

I shout, *"Estoy aquí!"*
I am strong.

I see white, soft clouds
I hear the wind
I taste bitterness
I feel cold
I think I am home.
I whisper *"Estás ahí?"*
I am migrant.

I want to go to college
I will graduate
I won't ever stop trying
I can see my future
I pretend I am not tired.

I sing in my mind
I am proud.

I dream awake
I am afraid of failure
I reach to the sky
I say I'm sorry when I fail
I love my life.

I declare for the world to hear that
I will rise like an eagle
I am a part of life.

Cilviana in front of the Washington Monument in Washington, DC

La Mata-Chickens
(The Chicken Killer)
Dictated by Teresa. 14 years old. June 2011

The first chicken I killed right, but I didn't cut the wings or the feet right. I used the *escoba* (broom) to kill it. Since that time, I've barely killed three. The first one was not good, the second one was all right, and the third one was good. I was so proud of myself because I cut the things right and I took the guts out, everything inside the body, and I had to be careful because there's a green thing and if it explodes it will make the chicken all sour and I took it out for the first time yesterday. Good thing I didn't pop it. If I pop it, my mom would get mad.

When I feel sorry for the chicken, my mom says, "Sorry chicken but you were born to die. *Que dios me perdone!*" I told my mom she should operate on people because she cuts good.

First I grab the escoba and put the chicken's head under the stick of the escoba, and then I put my foot on top of the escoba and then I grab the chicken's legs and I pull and that's it and it's dead. That squishes the chicken's neck and then we check the neck for a pulse. And then white stuff and blood comes out of the mouth. And you have to hold it upside down and tie the feet with a strip of the tortilla cloth.

First you kill it with the escoba, then you put it in hot water, then you take out the feathers, then you cut it, and then you take out everything inside, then you have to take off the *mugre* (dirt) with the *cuchillo* (kitchen knife) with cold water, and then you put it in the refrigerator.

I felt proud and excited because I killed and cut the chicken all by myself and I never, ever, ever did that. I never thought I was going to kill a chicken because my sister never did that, and she's nineteen. My mom said nice things, like, "You're not even Mexican and you know how to do this" (because I was born in California). And I said, "Of course I know how to do it, mom!"

Everything we do is called learning, learning from mistakes, because first I messed up with the first chicken, but then I learned and yesterday I cut a good chicken. The first chicken was only three weeks ago. I learn fast.

The following four essays were written as part of student applications for migrant scholarship to the U.S. Space Academy. Rosa won one of the scholarships in 2011 and spent one week studying with astronauts in Alabama.

My Goals for the Future
by Rosa. 12 years old. January 2011

Hello, my name is Rosa and I am a 7th grade student at Mount Baker Middle School in Mount Vernon, Washington.

My life as a migrant student is very hard. During the summer I go to work in the fields with my parents. I do not like working in the fields but I have to so my parents can get help with money. It is very hard working in the fields because I always have to wake up at 5:00 in the morning. When the summer is almost over I am happy because school is almost starting and I stop working in the fields.

My parents tell us that school is important and I agree about what my parents tell me. I enjoy going to school. School makes me feel like I want to learn more and cannot stop learning. I like school because it helps me. All the educational learning I will use in the future.

My goal in life is to graduate middle school and go to high school. I will get my diploma. I especially want to go to college. What I want to be when I grow up is to be a doctor. I want to be a doctor because I like helping others when they get sick.

My participation in school is that I am a Bilingual Peer Tutor. What I do in that class is help other students with their English. I like that class because some of the kids are learning English very fast. Another thing is I am involved in Migrant Girls' Club. What we do there is help each other and stay motivated to not drop out of school. I like it because Ms. Blackmore gives me good advice.

Sometimes I don't believe in myself but if I make it to Space Academy things will change because it will make me want to believe in myself. Thank you for your time and consideration.

Rosa (bottom right) and friends.

My Life as a Migrant
by Martha. 13 years old. February 2010

My name is Martha. I'm thirteen and attend LaVenture Middle School. I want to attend U.S. Space Academy because this is a one-time opportunity that will help my good reputation when I go to college, and it will make my family proud of me.

My life as a migrant has been working in the fields. For example, I have worked picking blueberry, strawberry, cucumbers, and doing other things in Washington since I was five or six years old every summer by helping out my parents. My mom never went to school, so she doesn't know how to write or read that good and sometimes I help her. One day she told me she wants me to do better at school, and not work in the fields like her. That's why she's here in the U.S., she told me. And she tells me to try hard and she'll help me in anyway she can. And this is a reason I want to go, also to prove to my parents I can be successful.

I like school. I think school is an important step to becoming successful in life, but I would like school to be more interesting. For example, during free time, put a lab where we could do chemistry and other subjects that have to do with science, and with adult supervision so we can learn things we can't learn during math or science class. I also don't want to waste teachers' time because in Mexico you have to pay for your education. In the U.S. it's free and the teachers do care about you, not like in Mexico where they sometimes don't really care. That's why I take school seriously, not like a joke.

My goals in life are to be a doctor, teacher, or interpreter, especially because I'm bilingual. I also chose these jobs because I like working with people and kids. One thing that motivates me is that I was watching the Spanish channel and I heard a guy from NASA say, "It takes a million steps to reach your dream, but you have to think positive."

I participate in Migrant Girls' Club. I'm in a sport, which is basketball, and I was in volleyball and soccer. Besides school, I participate outside of school like in Homework Club, Shark Club, I attend at church, I was in chorus, I also do childcare, and I'm in Youth Club. Next year I'm looking forward to participating more so I will have a good reputation when I go to college.

Well that's not everything, but hopefully this will help you decide that I really want to go and discover things I don't know of yet. Thank you for taking your time and reading my letter.

Martha at the U.S. Space Academy (bottom row, 4th from left)

My Family, My Challenges, My Life
by Verónica. 13 years old. February 2010

Hi! My name is Verónica L. I was born in Guerrero, Oaxaca. My family came to live in Zapata, Baja California. The school I went to was Ricardo Flores Magón. We lived with my uncle while my dad and mom came to work in the United State for a better life for us. We lived several years away from my parents but then we got back together in 2005. When we got back together, my mom had a new kid. It was a girl. Now my family is living in Mount Vernon. When I lived in Zapata, Spanish became my second language. I know now three languages, Mixteco, Spanish, and English. I have a big family. We are ten all together.

I have always liked school. I take school seriously. I am a smart girl. I always try my best at everything. When I go to school, I always think positively. I say to myself, "Today you are going to learn something new." It is very important for me to learn something new every day. The more I learn the better for me. I think when I grow up I want to be a teacher.

My family works in the fields. Every summer after school is over I have to go and work in the fields with my dad and sisters. We work in the strawberries, blackberries, and blueberries. It's always been hard for me to work in the fields and then come back to school because I never have time to read and study. I am always tired and exhausted.

My two older sisters that went to middle school didn't get a chance to go to Space Camp. My oldest sister didn't even get a chance to finish middle school. This will mean a lot to me because I can show my dad that I am a smart girl. This will be an awesome opportunity for me to meet new kids that are my age and that are migrant students like me.

I participated in soccer. Now I am playing basketball. At the school that I attend, I am in a club called Migrant Girls' Club. I have talked in the community about a movie called "Papers". We are trying to bring this movie to Mount Vernon.

My mom and dad both didn't go to school. So when I have homework they can't help because they don't know what the lesson is about. When I want to have free time to play sports, my family says no because my mom and dad think those are only for boys. I never like to wear dresses so everyone says to me that I look like a guy only because I am wearing pants. We girls weren't supposed to have boyfriends. I believe that this could be an opportunity to show my parents that we women can come a long way in life. I understand that in my culture women usually stay home and do housework, take care of the family, and the men work. I want to be able to accomplish many things in life and this would be one of them.

My biggest challenge is to go to school. My dad says that I will go to high school and that's all. I would love to go to a two-year collage then to a university. I have heard that people who are undocumented can't get a job even though they went to college. I pray that the DREAM Act is taken into consideration so that I can live up to my dreams of going to college and getting a good job.

I hope I have the opportunity to go to Space Camp. I will always be thankful to you for letting me participate in this event.

Verónica & friends with bandanas that read: "Support the DREAM Act"

Luis won one of the migrant scholarships to the U.S. Space Academy in 2011. He also won a migrant scholarship for a week in Washington, DC that same summer.

My Migrant Life and Goals
by Luis. 14 years old. January 2011

There have been many things I have wanted to do, things that I've only dreamed of but couldn't do because of my family being a migrant family and working in agriculture. I hear other kids talking about trips and when they ask me where I've been I just say nothing because I can't. I have not been anywhere besides my town and close little places. So I want to go to the U.S. Space Academy Space and Rocket Center because I want to make my family proud. I really want to show kids and people that I am capable of doing great things. Just because I am a migrant does not mean I can't achieve anything. I want to reach high. Another reason I want to go is to make my family proud. No one in my family has ever done something like this so I really want to go and be the first!

First of all my life as a migrant has been very, very hard, moving from school to school, barely learning new concepts. Sometimes I finally get settled and we have to move again. I really do not like this although I understand why. My parents always say, "We are really sorry but you know we have to move to survive. When you grow up I want you to be something so you don't have to live like this." So today the reason I get up in the morning is because I want an education. My attitude towards school is great. I really enjoy learning new things. In fact, I am in a class called AVID. It stands for Advancement Via Individual Determination. That's what I am – a determined student wanting a better future.

My goals in life are very big. I have a big dream! I really want to be a computer and information scientist because I really like working with computers and I like making and working with programs. I have heard that computer scientists work with robotics, and to me that is fascinating! Another reason is because some people say that's impossible. I take impossible as a reason to try harder! A reason I want to go is because this might help me get into a good university, so I have a fighting chance to succeed in this world.

My interest in science and math is that I really enjoy them. I enjoy math because I get challenged on some problems, which is fun, and it motivates me. Some kids say math is hard, but I just do it because life is going to be even harder, so I have to work hard. I also really enjoy science a lot because I get to do many experiments and learn lots of cool things. Sometimes I daydream about all the cool inventions I could make when I become a scientist.

My participation in school and family and community is great. In school, when my friends need help with their homework I help them. In AVID we have something called tutorials. It is where you help other kids by asking them questions. It's like I am the teacher helping kids. Also I really don't want my little sister to go through all the same ups and downs that I have gone through, so I help her with her reading and homework. I do this because I want my sister to be an outstanding student! Some of my community activities I do are that I have a class called Grizzly Club where we had a food drive, made brochures for people who are looking for help, and donated clothes for the needy. Also we wrote letters to Congress. I wrote to President Barack Obama about how they should pass the Child Nutrition Reauthorization Bill.

If I get chosen, I will benefit in many ways. It will really impact my life. I will always remember and encourage other migrants to apply to the Space and Rocket Center. I also really want to go because it can increase my knowledge in math and science and life, also by seeing new things. Finally this might help me get into the university of my choice, which is Yale. I truly hope you consider my application!

Luis (on left) and friends in front of the Washington Monument.

Wrong To Worse But Then To Better
by Yolanda. 14 years old. December 2011

As my eyes grow tired and I begin to feel faded
Mommy strokes my hair, proud of what she created.
She whispers in my small ear, "Mommy's pride and joy,"
She promises me happiness and a lot of toys.

Although I was small, I still knew her words were lies,
I understood what pain was and I knew what were cries.
At my age it was surprising what I knew
But I learned words and definitions as I grew.
I learned them by feeling or hearing things at home.
I learned what fear was when dad was drunk and I was alone.
I learned what pain was and how it felt
Anytime I made dad angry he would strike me with his belt.
I learned that nightmares reveal your fears and your feelings,
I would have flashbacks of dad's screams and beatings.

At the age of six I learned that cruelty is power
If I refused to obey they would soak me clothed in a cold shower.
I learned *pendeja* meant something bad
Cause dad would use it anytime he was mad.
I learned that forgiving was forgetting things that you felt or heard,
Dad would change his attitude and forget about everything that occurred.

I learned what hate was at the age of nine.
Dad would blame me for things I didn't do, it was never anyone else's fault,
it was mine.

At the age of ten my new word was retaliation
I wanted to get back at mom and dad for the times I got hit and never
received appreciation.
Another word was homies, they're people who understood me,
Accepted who I was, we had things in common, we agreed.
My favorite word at the time was marijuana, it helped me forget if I
couldn't on my own.
I learned how to use it, how to get it, and how it was grown

At the age of eleven I learned the words dangerous and overdose.
Marijuana was helpful but also lead you wrong, your life could close.
Then I learned love meant many things,
Just to have my homie still alive, I would give anything.

Then there were the words death and sorrow.
Can't fiddle with one's life cause its not something you can borrow.
At the age of twelve I learned the word regret.
I heard and saw people who I wish I never met.

At the age of thirteen the drugs were doing me wrong,
Got caught up in conflicts, started relying on my bong.

At the age of fourteen I learned the words lost and rebellious.
My mom noticed me acting strange, no longer serious.
Things started falling apart, I could no longer take it.
The truth spilled out, my mom now knew, and I didn't deny it.
Things got better, when I looked for help there were no longer beatings
The anger and insults were now over and so was the screaming
Things went from wrong to worse but then to better,
Mrs. Blackmore helped me…I'm thankful I met her.

Eres Tu
(It's You)
by Alma. 13 years old. June 2009

Quise alcanzar las estrellas
Pero mis manos ya estaban llenas
Quise dejarme vencer
Pero tu no me dejaste caer.

Gracias por preocuparte de mi
Nadie ocupará el lugar que ocupas aquí
Me nombraste tu estrella
Tu eres la razón que yo pude llegar allá
No te digo adiós
Yo te digo "Nos veremos".

Dame tu buena suerte
Y espero que me haga más fuerte
Por el momento
Por favor recibe esto.

I wanted to reach the stars
But my hands were already full
I wanted to give up
But you didn't let me fall.

Thank you for caring about me
Nobody will hold the place that you
hold here
You called me your star
You are the reason that I could
make it there.
I am not telling you goodbye
I am just telling you we'll see each
other soon

Give me your good luck
And I hope it'll make me stronger
For now
Please receive this poem.

Alma and Ms. Blackmore's daughter, Luna

Me Llaman Vivi
(They Call Me Vivi)
by Viviana. 14 years old. April 2010

I am Viviana *y me llaman Vivi.*

I was born in Santa Maria, California, and lived there almost all my life.

My familia showed me to respect and to learn to be clean.

As a little girl, I always sang wherever I went.

Es importante tener el valor de no fallar and get *una vida* that I deserve.

My family has love for each other, *muchísimo para siempre.*

I am Viviana *y me llaman Vivi.*

My strength is to be strong.

I dream of *una casa grande* with 2 floors and a long *escalera.*

My hope is to get a good job with a brave attitude.

Cuando sea grande,

I want to become a good *enfermera* for all my people.

People should believe in the trust and love for you and me.

I am Viviana *y me llaman Vivi.*

Prison
Nico. 14 years old. April 2012

They want to send me to prison. When I say "they", I mean the *güeros*, the white people. I'm not racist but I'm just saying what I feel.

I'm going to tell you the story of my life; it's all true. It's the story of a migrant kid's life. Not all migrant kids live through the same thing as me, but quite a few do.

Some people think we migrant people are like animals, but we're not; we're humans too. We have feelings.

I was not born in the U.S. I was born in Sonora, Mexico, but I never got to see it because my mom crossed the border with me as a baby. She got caught and got locked up with me in her arms. Then she eventually crossed again and made it to our first home in Southern California.

When we got to the U.S. we were seven people in my family, counting my parents. Then my mom got pregnant again and had my younger brother. While she was pregnant with him the doctors told her that after she had him they were going to operate on her so she wouldn't have more kids, but my dad told them not to get rid of the future babies because it was a blessing for him to have kids so they did not get rid of them. Then my mom had another baby in Southern California and one more once we moved to Mount Vernon, Washington.

When we got here to Washington, my parents both got a job at the same place. Every summer when school finished my family would work in the fields and, from a young age, I would too. By the time the work finished, it was time for school again.

As I grew older and older, I began to get involved with not-the-best-kind of people and I would do not-so-good things in school.

At the age of ten or eleven my dad died of cancer and my life changed.

Since then I've been getting into a lot of trouble in and out of school. I have made my mom and other family members cry because of my mistakes and now I'm in deep trouble with the law. I messed up in school and now I have to pay the consequences. I'm scared I could end up in prison. I spent twelve days in the Juvenile Detention Center. I begged my family to forgive me, so they did. I would have spent a longer time in "juvi" but my mom and older brother bailed me out. However, my lawyer told me I still have a chance of going to prison. I think it's possible because the prosecutor made some racist comments in the courtroom, accusing me of hurting a citizen of his community. Aren't I a citizen of this community too?

People look at me all the time in stores because they think I might steal something because of the way I dress. Before I went to "juvi" I did not care what I did or what happened to me, but now I do. Now that I'm out because of my mom and brother, I plan to change.

Yesica and Lucía

Brown and Proud
by Yesica and Lucía. 14 and 15 years old. May 2011

The color of my eyes and skin are brown
I am proud of my race so don't put it down
I come from a place where people have dreams
A place real poor where the sun still beams
I come from Mexico and its lovely spaces
I have respect for all the world's races.

Children wishing on a star at night
Watching the stars shine real bright
There are people laughing and people shedding tears
People don't care people just don't hear.

Keep your head up when something tries to stop your dream
Be true to yourself and keep on dreaming.

*Submitted and selected for a Migrant Student Leadership Conference T-shirt, symboliz-
ing the upward flight of struggling migrant students.*

The Dove
by an Anonymous Male Student. 14 years old. May 2009

Since I Was Five – a Rap
by Eber. 13 years old. May 2011

Crossing the border is hard as you can see.
This life of an immigrant is a hard life for me.
I came here when I was five.
I've tried hard to survive
In this new world I've come to hold.
I started school in the second grade.
I was not scared, wasn't afraid.
Here I learned a new language and to move on.
This is why I am rapping this song.
I work hard in the fields
To earn some of my meals.
I struggled a lot in my Californian school.
My teacher took me for a fool.
I did not pass fifth grade.
I am trying for the past to fade.
I've been through a lot of racism and discrimination
But I did not pay any attention.
Every year I work in the fields
But that part of my life is almost sealed.
I have a future ahead of me.
I know what I want to do, what I want to be.
I have found new friends and a new life.
My life has changed since I was five.

I, Too, Sing America

By Langston Hughes
Selected by Julio. 15 years old. December 2011

I, too, sing America.

I am the darker brother.
They send me to eat in the kitchen
When company comes,
But I laugh,
And eat well,
And grow strong.

Tomorrow,
I'll be at the table
When company comes.
Nobody'll dare
Say to me,
'Eat in the kitchen,'
Then.

Besides,
They'll see how beautiful I am
And be ashamed--

I, too, am America.

I Am Migrant

Lucía and Teresa. 15 years old. December 2011

I am migrant
I won't deny it
I will light it.

Migrants with education
And determination
It's just getting people's attention.

I am brown and proud
Don't make a crowd
Let's all spread around
To be found
In our town
No matter what goes down.

La migra va y viene
Pasa pero nunca nos detiene
Tengo sed no hay nada que hacer
Hay muchos coyotes que prometer
Pero nunca cumplen
Lo que nos ofrecen
So no se sienten
ni enfrenten
Lo que viene en su frente.

I am Mexican
It runs through my veins
That's how I've been raised
No matter what people say

No sabemos medir
Sabemos vivir
Sabemos estudiar
Sabemos luchar
So no hay que engañar
Por eso vinimos a este mundo para
ganar.

I am migrant
I won't deny it
I will light it.

Tengo mi familia
Pero no tenemos envidia
El dios me dio una vida
Para vivirla.

Las personas nos buscan
para hacer justicia
Y decir cosas de racista
En el futuro quiero ser
alguien en el mundo
Para tener todo mi grupo junto
Y si no los dejan cruzar
Nos lo va a ir mal
Por eso voy a estudiar
Para vivir en paz.

I am migrant
I won't deny it
I will light it.

Index

A

Agustín 15
Alejandro I. 55
Alejandro R 92
Alma 100, 112
Alondra 15
Angelina 64
Ann Nolan Clark 55
Anonymous 20, 39, 40, 44, 117
Antonio 36

C

Carl Bruner 23
Carolina G. 78
Carolina S. 13, 65
Celia 61, 67, 75
Cilviana 10, 101

D

Daniel Galán 64

E

Eber 57, 95, 118
Elia Solís 67
Elissa 9, 84
Elizabeth R. 90
Elizabeth S. 89, 96
Emily Martin 80
Exell 35, 66

F

Fidel 7, 16
Frank 18, 24, 50, 60

G

Guadalupe 54, 60

H

Heather Goodrich 67, 70

J

Janet 98
Janice Blackmore xiii, 26, 52, 86
Jasmine 14
Jesús 59
Jesús Guillen 47
John M. Crisp 22
Jonathan 9, 14

José 65
Julian 17
Julio 25, 32, 119

L

Langston Hughes 119
LaVenture Middle School 68, 70, 86, 99, 104
Lucía 116, 120
Luis 108

M

Martha 104
Mayra 8, 64
Migrant Leaders Club xii, 2, 3, 4, 27, 68
Moisés 53, 60
Monserrat 74
Mount Baker Middle School 23, 54, 103
Mount Vernon School Board 23

N

Nico 114

R

Rigoberto 41
Roberto 48, 49, 66
Rogelia 7
Rosa 103
Rosie 68
Ruby 14

S

Shane Koyczan 82
Shannon Saylor 99

T

Tania 23
Teresa 10, 48, 56, 102, 120
Thalía 82
Tina 72, 76

V

Verónica 11, 13, 106
Viviana 113
Vladimir 51, 62

Y

Yesica 10, 31, 42, 79, 116
Yolanda 110

Made in the USA
San Bernardino, CA
10 March 2013